Two Worlds: Above and Below the Sea
David Doubilet

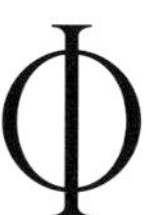

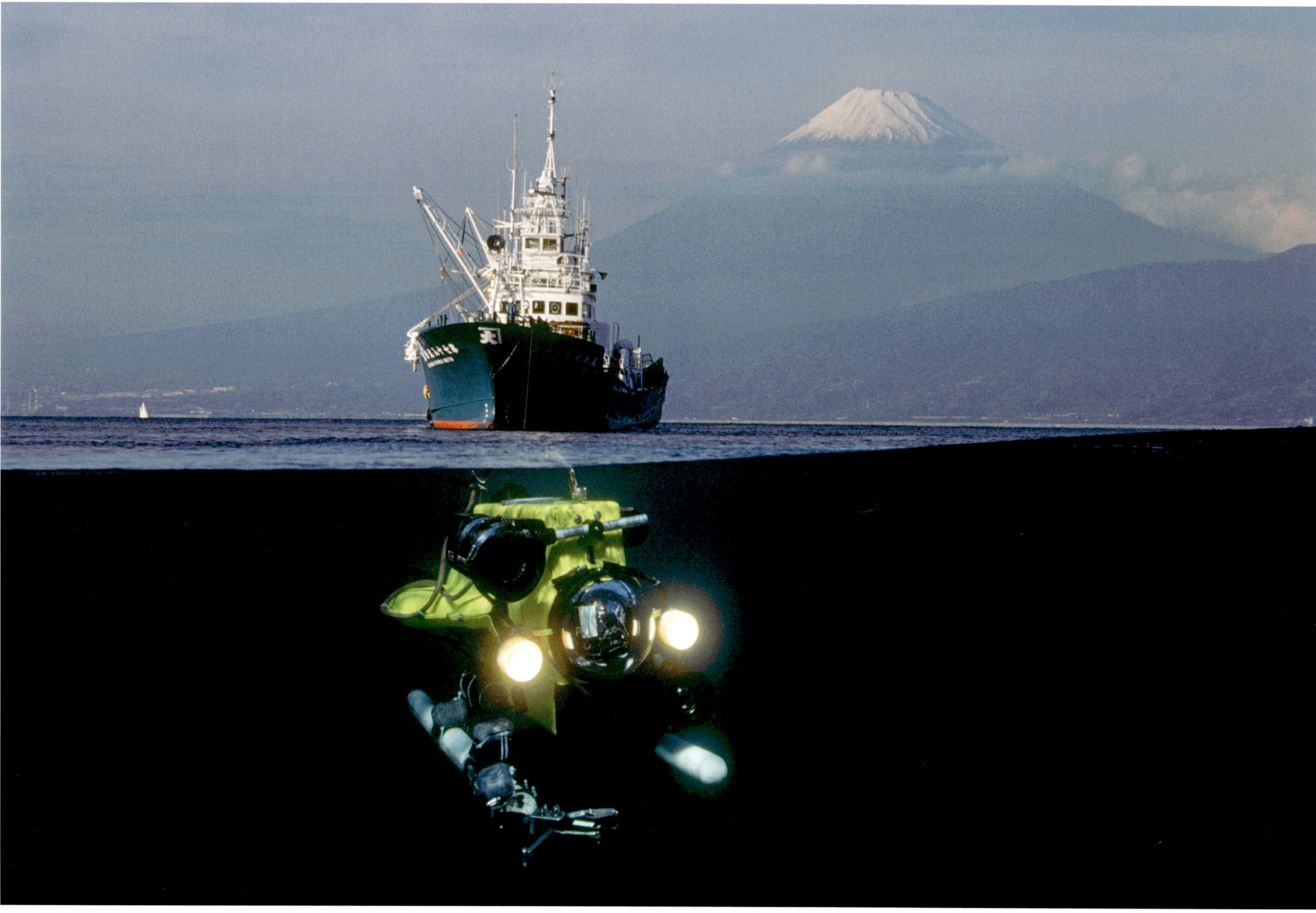

Preface
by David Doubilet

As a *National Geographic* photographer, I have been granted the priceless perspective of time in our oceans. When I began making images underwater, we felt the seas were infinite and invincible – but subtle, and then cataclysmic, environmental changes have reshaped that reality. The gift of storytelling not only came with unique opportunities for exploration and encounters, but also with the emotional burden of my work being a visual testimony to this passage of time. Looking back, I realize the images bear witness to the wonder, the beauty, the loss and, I hope, the resilience of our oceans. I photograph now with a sense of purpose, urgency and, yes, poetry. In my head and heart, it is critical to make a picture that transcends journalism, to create an image that reaches into the realm of art. If we lose the sense of hope and magic in the sea, we have lost all.

I discovered that magic at nine years old, when I meticulously planned and executed a perilous circumnavigation around the jetty that stretched from the Ocean Beach Club in Elberon, New Jersey, into the wild Atlantic. I can report that the mysterious green waters did not disappoint. My Frankie the Frogman flippers propelled me through schools of silversides as wary tautogs peered from the shadows. I surfaced just enough to glimpse the world below and the world above, where I realized the lifeguard was angrily blowing his whistle and demanding that I return to shore. I made two important discoveries that day that sank deep into my nine-year-old neurons. First, I could exist in two realms at once, and second, I could disappear into the world below and leave the noise behind.

In the fall of 1956, Captain Jacques-Yves Cousteau's film *The Silent World* opened in New York City – I was mesmerized. I bought the book, then read and re-read it (usually under the covers at night with a Rayovac flashlight) with the devotion of a young Rabbinical scholar. Cousteau described his first real look into the sea, while wearing Maurice Fernez-patented goggles, in 1936: 'standing up to breathe, I saw a trolley car, people, electric light poles. I put my head back underwater and civilization vanished with one last bow'. Cousteau had distilled into words my vision of 'two worlds'.

It would take 15 years and a revolutionary photographic advance to capture this vision on film. Making underwater pictures in the 1950s and '60s was monstrously frustrating. I could see wide-angle scenes but could not make them. Furthermore, the pre-historic housings I used offered a choice between focus and exposure, but never both. I was grateful that black-and-white film had a forgiving range. In 1969, *National Geographic* photographer Bates Littlehales and engineer Gomer McNeill designed the 'Ocean Eye', an underwater housing with a large acrylic dome. This invention was a game-changer and made my career possible. I could begin to make the images of which I had dreamed and capture that extraordinary window between the air and water.

This book is a personal journey. Secretly, these half-and-half images represent my lifelong escape from the reality of the surface. As an asthmatic who disliked most sports, I did not have a stellar childhood on land. Underwater was sheer unfettered joy, a place where I could be myself and let my curiosity run wild. It was a land where the bizarre was commonplace, and the surreal was a given.

Dreams born off that jetty inspired me to seek a life in photography, one that would allow me to work beneath the most important border on our planet – the magical molecular boundary separating surface and sea. My partner, photographer and biologist Jennifer Hayes, and I go beneath the surface to tell a story. On each assignment, I endeavour to create a half-and-half image that captures the essence of that place at that time. These frames are elusive, but when they do happen, they give the story another dimension and provide an unexpected view of two worlds.

Pictures are a universal language, one that has the power to honour, educate, celebrate, humiliate and illuminate. Photography can open people's eyes, minds and hearts to new worlds. These photographs invite you to look through the surface, imagine, dream and come to know the sea.

As the oceans go, so do we.

We live on a water planet. We breathe in a sea of air, while around us is a sea of water. The divide is razor-thin, but few of us will ever experience both realms and understand the planet in its totality. Those who do slip under the water's surface usually focus on what is beneath. Isn't that the goal, after all? To look down and around, and leave our world behind. To swim with schools of fish, sharks and marine mammals; to glide over beds of seagrass, marvel at gardens of coral, dare to swim under ice and into caves, or float above the abyss. The sheer audacity of breathing underwater would be enough to know that your world had expanded beyond imagining. But when you put it all together, it is nothing short of miraculous. The embrace of the water, the diversity, the otherworldliness of being under the sea – a place so different that it deserves its own language.

I can dive. I have experienced the shiver of having a shark swim near, the giddiness that comes with spotting a turtle before it rockets away, the tickle of being surrounded by fish and the awe of feeling the reverberation of a humpback's song. But I don't take to the water with ease. I am, as I think most of us are, a creature of the edge. I love being by the ocean. The salt air, the lash of the waves, the occasional glimpse of a fin breaking the surface and the great dark mystery of what lies beneath make me feel alive in a way that no mountain or forest ever could. Mountains contain; forests obscure; oceans expand. The water draws me close. Still, I prefer that edge and dipping a toe rather than full immersion. I remain tethered to the air. I do not speak the language of the sea.

David Doubilet not only speaks this language fluently, but he is also a poet of the sea. He has created an entirely new sort of image, one that reveals the tension and the wonder between the two worlds. He has found the space where water meets air, and his photographs interpret the merging – and the connectivity – of these worlds. He has framed the familiar and the alien. He has abolished the edge. His is a dynamic language, full of wonder, generosity and the fierce intent to share what he loves most. It is a language that has been crafted through decades of technical challenges, countless hours in the water

and a lyrical way of seeing. Because David does not just photograph: he sees, he feels and he speaks.

Above all, David is a storyteller, and every photograph in this book delivers a narrative in a single frame. The crest of a wave reveals a wealth of plate corals on Opal Reef in Australia (page 71). An iceberg seen above and below then pulls the eye toward the living art of glaciers in Scoresby Sund (pages 115–117). An American crocodile in the Gardens of the Queen in Cuba (page 34) is perfectly balanced between seagrass and mangroves, its reflection anchoring it to both worlds. A blast of flash at dusk exposes a frenzy of lemon sharks in the Bahamas (page 45). Each image is a story unto itself. You need nothing more to understand the diversity of a healthy reef, the raw power of a calving glacier and the supreme confidence of apex predators in their environments. It is there in the visual whisper.

David's understanding of what he wants to share is what shapes his approach. Yes, the equipment matters. Of course, you must master the physics of the air–water interface, but that is the background noise of technology and mathematics. First, one must ask, how do you tell a story? How do you make it memorable? All of the elements came together at North Sound, Grand Cayman Island (page 29). This is where David feels he made his first remarkable photograph merging two worlds. The earlier work was a novelty, stumbling toward this new language. But here, sky, sea, stingray, a dose of serendipity and David's visual sensibility join up to create a moment in the water. The curve of the ray's wing mirrors the sweep of the wave, while the chaos of the clouds creates a tension with the serenity of the sand. This is about seeing, understanding and patience. This is about storytelling.

The challenge of learning the language of the over and under is that the technique is inherently static. It must be understood, then discarded. To become fluent is to appreciate that a straight line is rarely the goal. That hard divide between land and sea is not the story. Nature flows, and so must language. It is the movement of the water, the balance between extremes, the energy that flows between both worlds that tells the story. David finds the dialogue between these two worlds and interprets it for us. Sometimes there is harmony, other times strife, often delight, but the narrative is always true to the story that must be told. Consider the echoing between a fjord in Gros Morne National Park in Newfoundland (page 59), rocks rising underwater in imitation of the mountains ringing the shoreline, with both worlds reflected in the water as if in conversation. Or the hidden riches of a coral reef in Kimbe Bay, seemingly revealed only to us as in a fairytale, while a fisherman and his son glide over the surface (page 105). Or the tragedy of climate change in Tumon Bay in Guam: dead coral exposed by the curl of the waves, our complicity evidenced by the hotels lurking in the background (pages 80–81). Each photograph is rich with its own story.

The connection between the two worlds is David's signature visual voice. If he was not the first to capture the play between over and under, he is the photographer who perfected the approach. David is known for bringing light into the sea, for adopting a street photographer's attitude toward documenting moments underwater, but the ability to merge two worlds is uniquely his. Many photographers now use the split (a word that David abhors as too harsh to speak of the sea), but few come close to his perfect blending of necessary technique and critical understanding of the language between sea, sky and land.

Like so many languages today, this visual coda that David has perfected is under threat. Reefs are bleaching, ice is melting, oceans are being overfished, and plastic can be found in the deepest canyons. But the photographs, the visual narratives in this book, remind us of why we care. They underscore the radiance just below the surface and how integral it is to all life – and, crucially, what we stand to lose if we let this language, this blending of our two worlds slip away. The story would end. Then there would be silence in the sea. Let's hope that never happens.

Suruga Bay, Japan, 1989 (page 4)

A remote-operated vehicle (ROV) controlled by *National Geographic*
colleague Emory Kristof begins its descent to explore Suruga Bay, a place
of earthly extremes. Japan's deepest bay plunges 2,500 metres (8,202
feet) into the abyss in the shadow of Mount Fuji, which soars 3,700 metres
(12,100 feet) above its surface. This picture presented unique optical
challenges to keep the size relationships true, balancing normal views above
the surface and wide-angle below. *National Geographic* photo-engineer
Kenji Yamaguchi and I devised a strategy to create an in-camera double
exposure that kept the imperial mountain majestic within the frame.

Chinstrap and Gentoo Penguins, Danco Island, Antarctica, 2011

A group of chinstrap (*Pygoscelis antarctica*) and gentoo (*Pygoscelis
papua*) penguins rest on a small iceberg called a bergy bit near Danco
Island, Antarctica. I was mesmerized by these Chaplinesque birds and
their conversations as I swam alongside their small island of ice. Both
species feed on declining populations of shrimp-like krill, but the gentoo
have adapted to a more diverse diet, allowing their numbers to expand
as chinstrap densities decline.

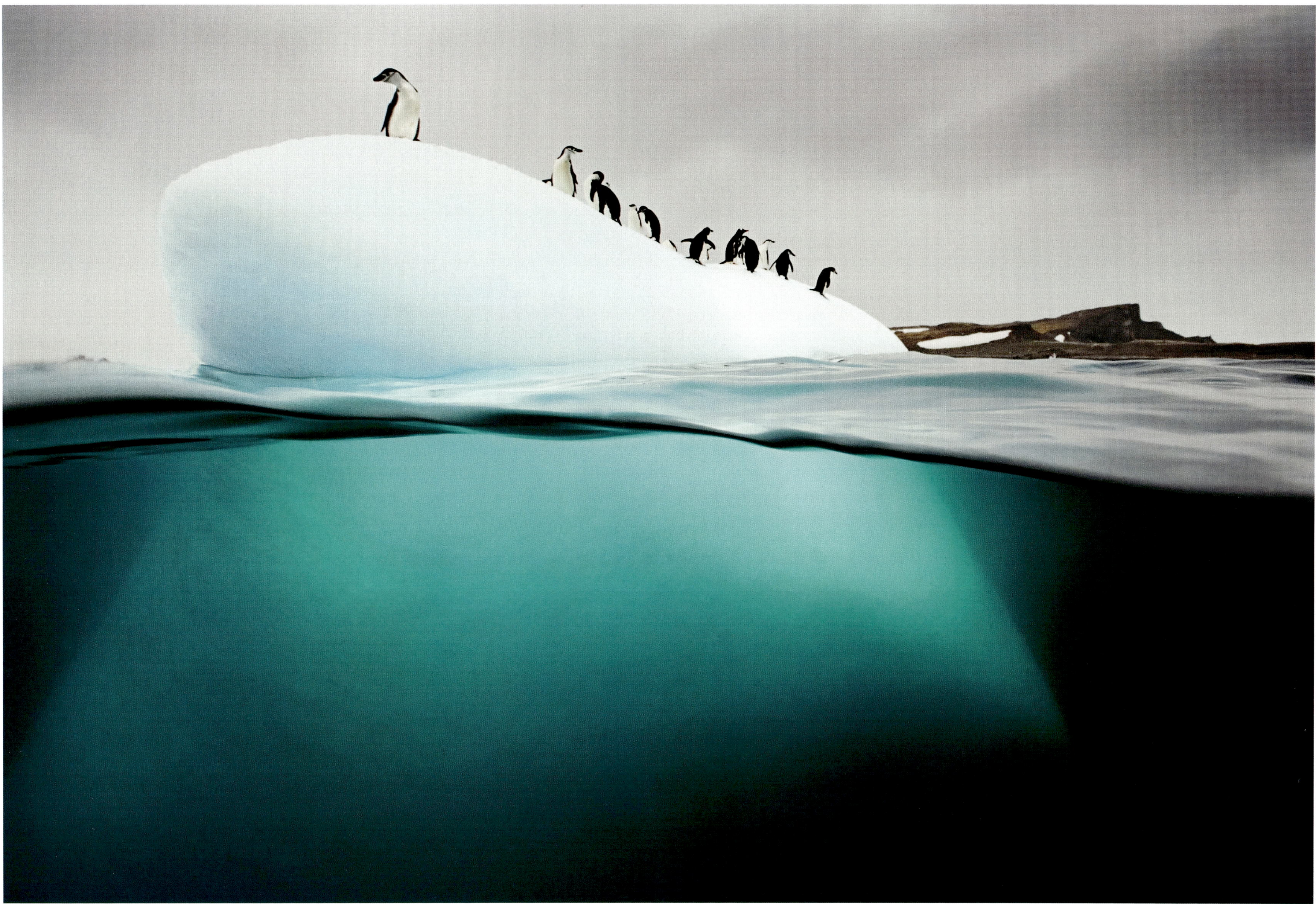

Chinstrap and Gentoo Penguins, Danco Island, Antarctica, 2011

On a grey, overcast day, we found a group of chinstrap and gentoo
penguins sharing a bergy bit near Danco Island. At first, they were wary,
thinking that I could be the enemy – a leopard seal. After a few minutes,
a chinstrap nudged a gentoo into the sea in front of me. The little penguin
zoomed past and leapt safely back onto the ice. The game 'King of the
Iceberg' was on. I watched as they slapped each other with their flippers,
tumbled into the water and flew like jets around the island, popping up
on the other side. I had dreamed of this picture since I was a kid wandering
through the Museum of Natural History in New York City.

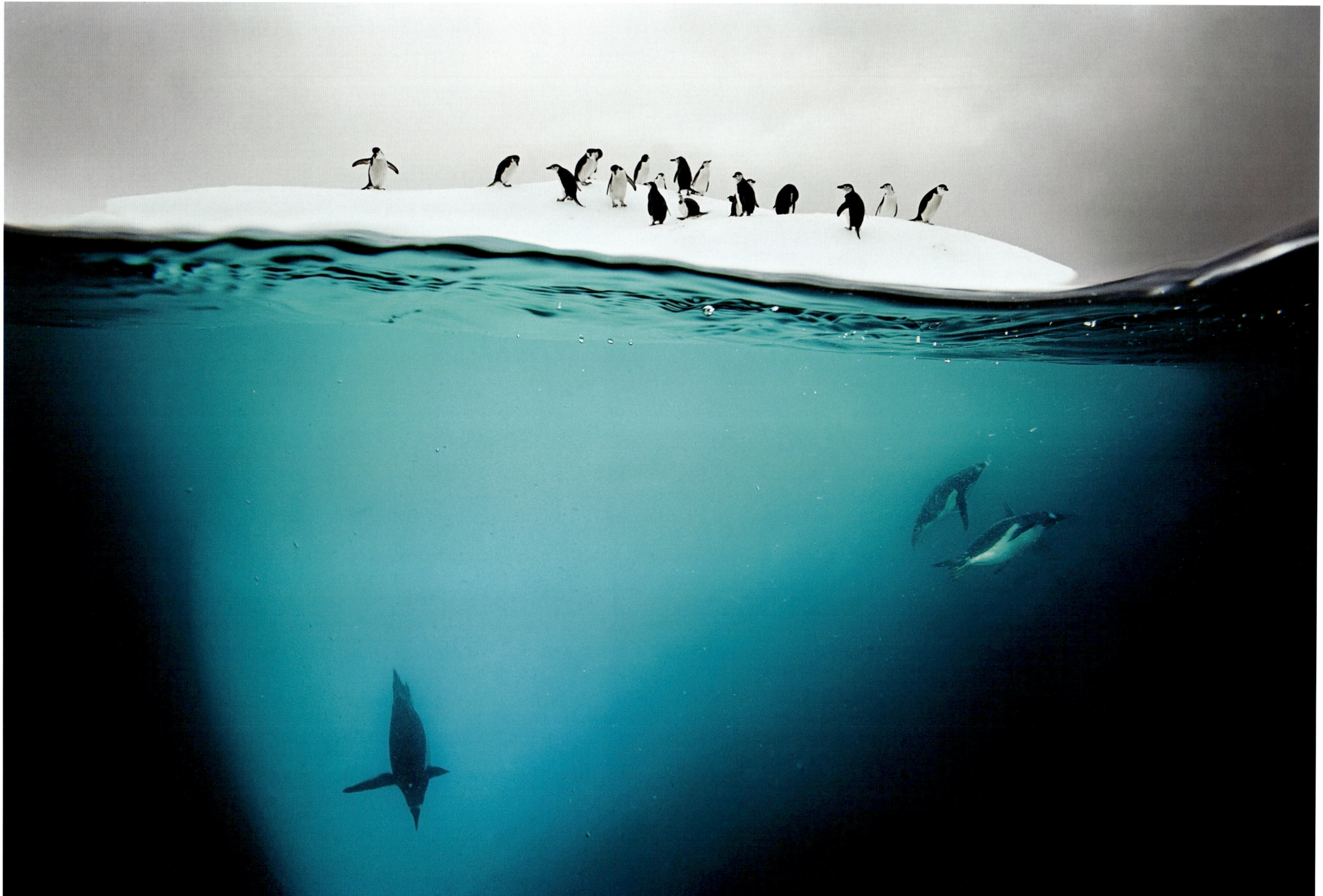

Iceberg, Antarctica, 2011

Icebergs are elusive. I rarely see the whole form because they may be
too large or the water too murky. To make this photograph, I swam
backward until I could see the entire iceberg and the mountain behind
it. I think of icebergs as a metaphor for the ocean because only a small
percentage is visible to the human eye.

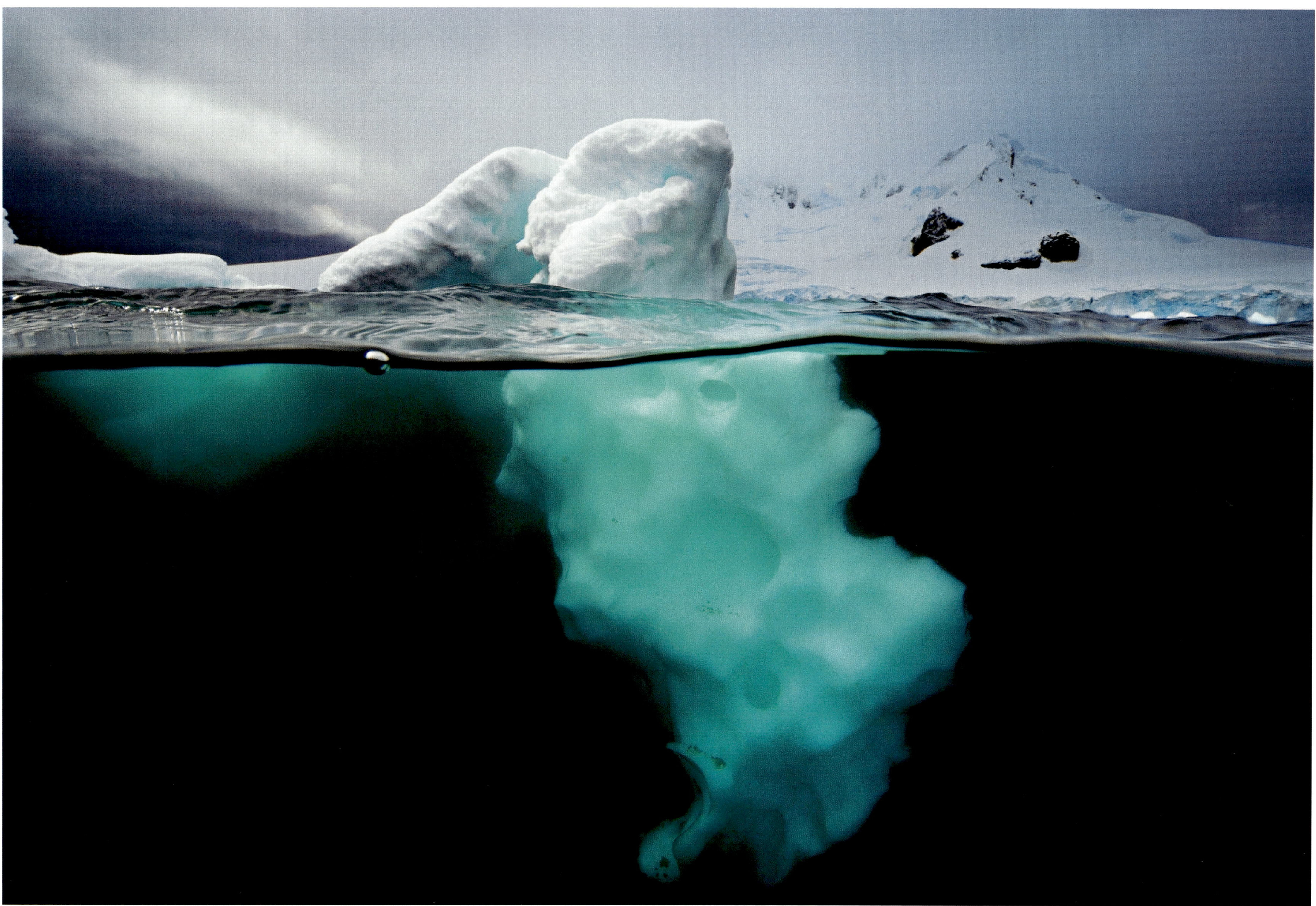

Iceberg and Zodiac, Antarctica, 2013

This nature-carved iceberg seems to dwarf the Zodiac boat beside it.
Wind and wave have created an abstract sculpture above the surface of
the sea that will soon disappear, leaving only the amorphous base below.
In Antarctica, we come for the creatures but are seduced by the ice.

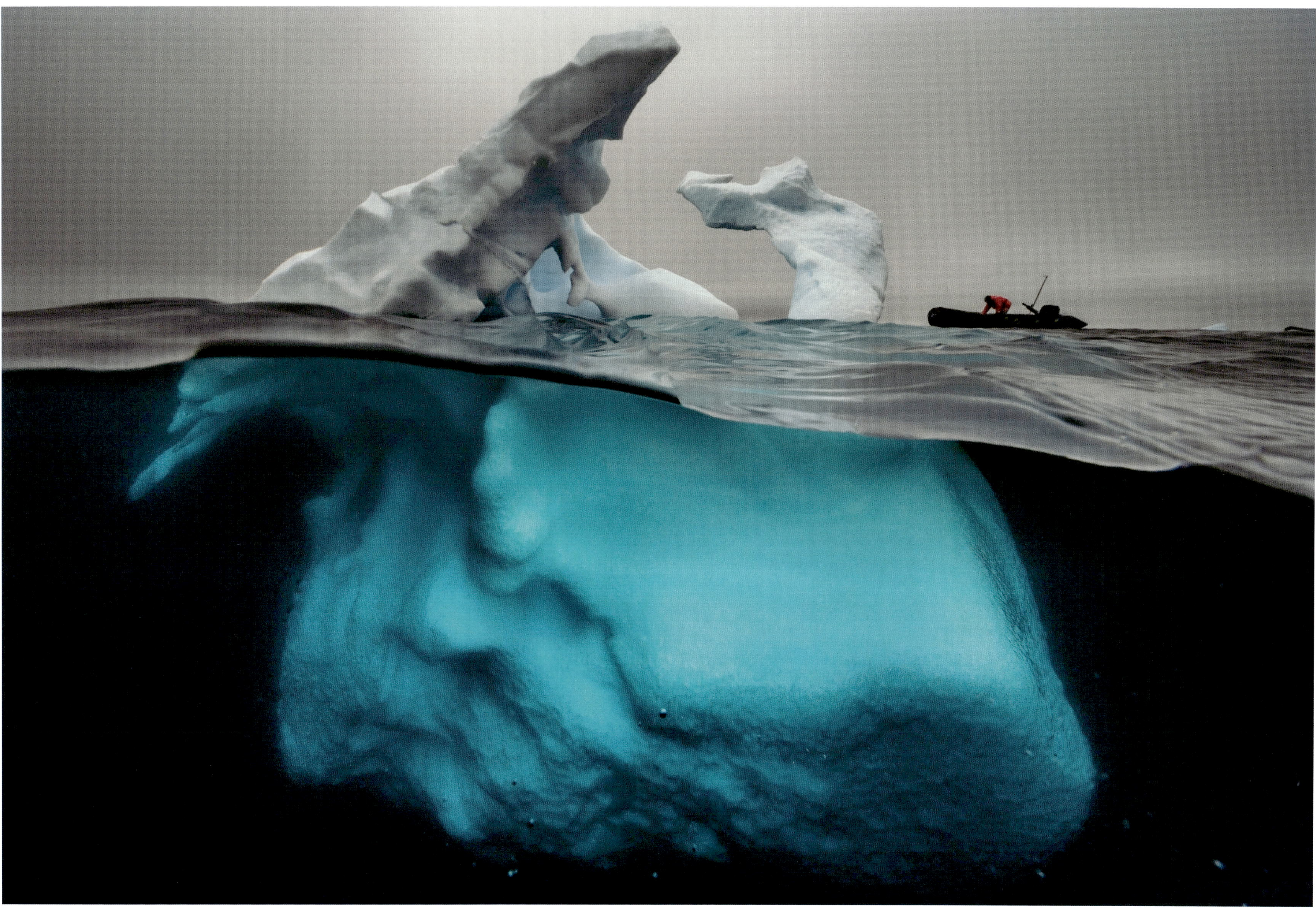

'Governoren,' Foyn Harbour, Enterprise Island, Antarctica, 2011

The rusted hull of the 'Governoren', shrouded in sea ice, rises defiantly against the snow-covered shores of Enterprise Island. The Norwegian whaler was celebrating the end of a successful hunting season when it caught fire in 1915, coming to permanent rest and ruin – a harsh reminder of the whaling era that hunted those gentle giants.

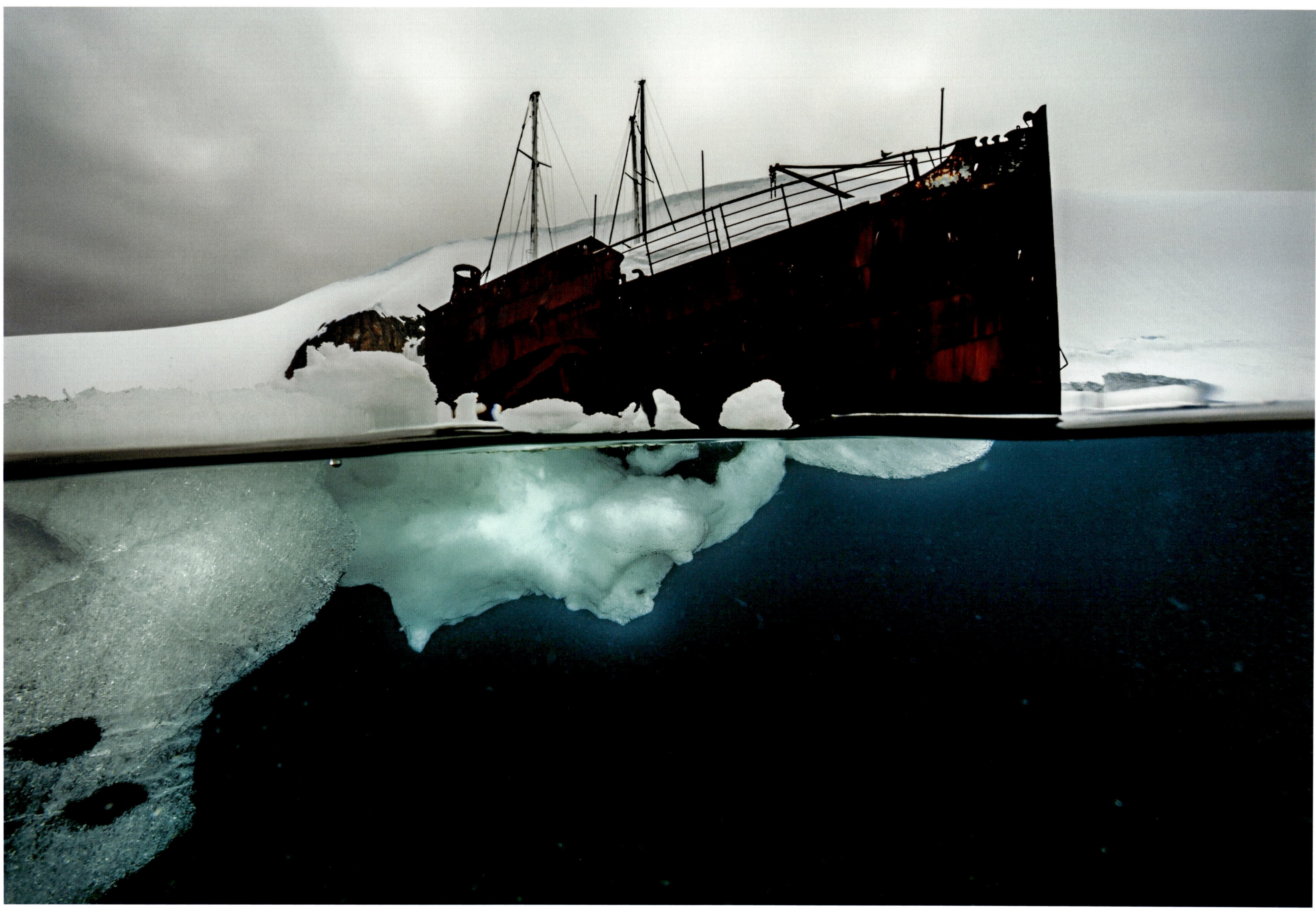

I snorkelled past a slumbering crabeater seal (*Lobodon carcinophagus*) on its own ice island. It detected my presence and yawned, exposing its special teeth for eating krill (despite their name, these wonderful creatures do not feast on crabs). I managed a single portrait before it fell asleep again.

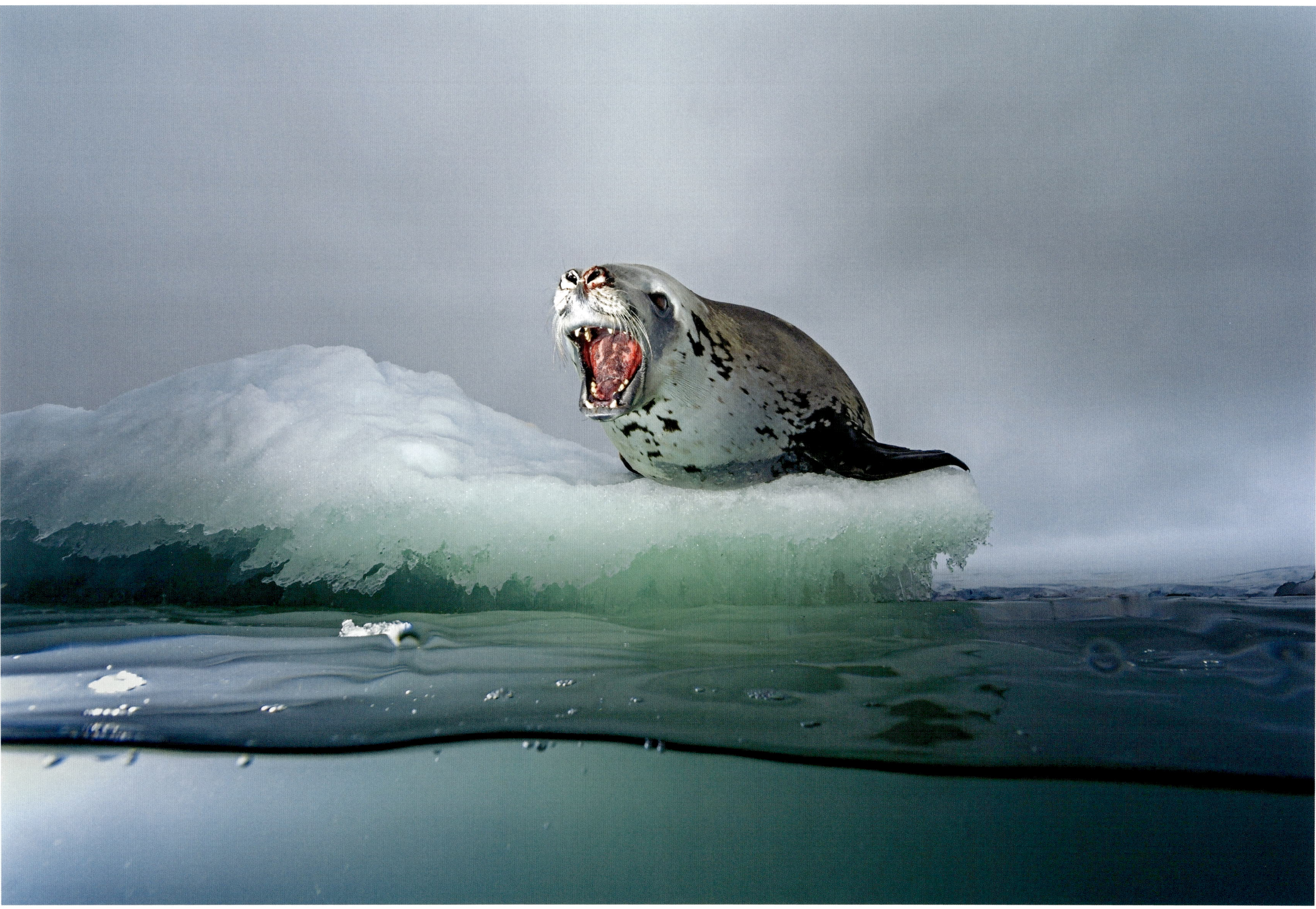

Iceberg Graveyard, Pleneau Bay, Antarctica, 2011

Emerald, plankton-rich waters veil the ghostly base of a blue iceberg
grounded in Pleneau Bay, Antarctica. The shallow bay is known as an
iceberg graveyard, where drifting icebergs become trapped and sculpted
by nature's unseen hand. It is a continually changing polar art gallery.

Antarctic Cormorants, Paradise Bay, Antarctica, 2016
(overleaf, left and right)

A juvenile Antarctic cormorant (*Leucocarbo bransfieldensis*, overleaf left)
landed on the water's surface next to me and watched my every move
while I photographed the noisy colony on the ledge above. The curious
bird could not resist pulling on loose straps and strobe cords. I discovered
they are graceful subjects and humorous snorkelling companions. Another
cormorant (overleaf right) guards its personal space against intruders.
Juveniles attempting to share the icy perch were met with a dodging dance
and flapping wings.

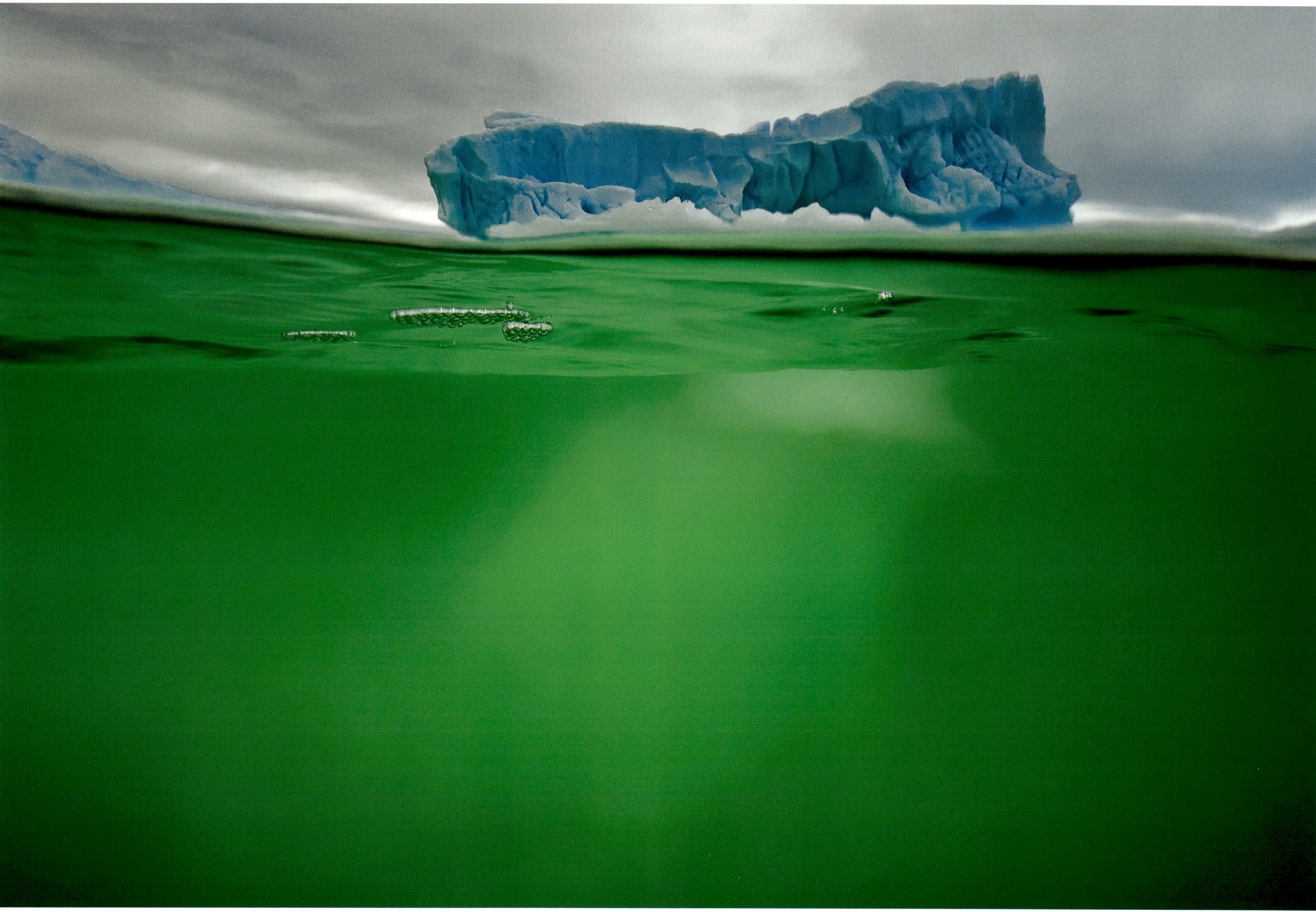

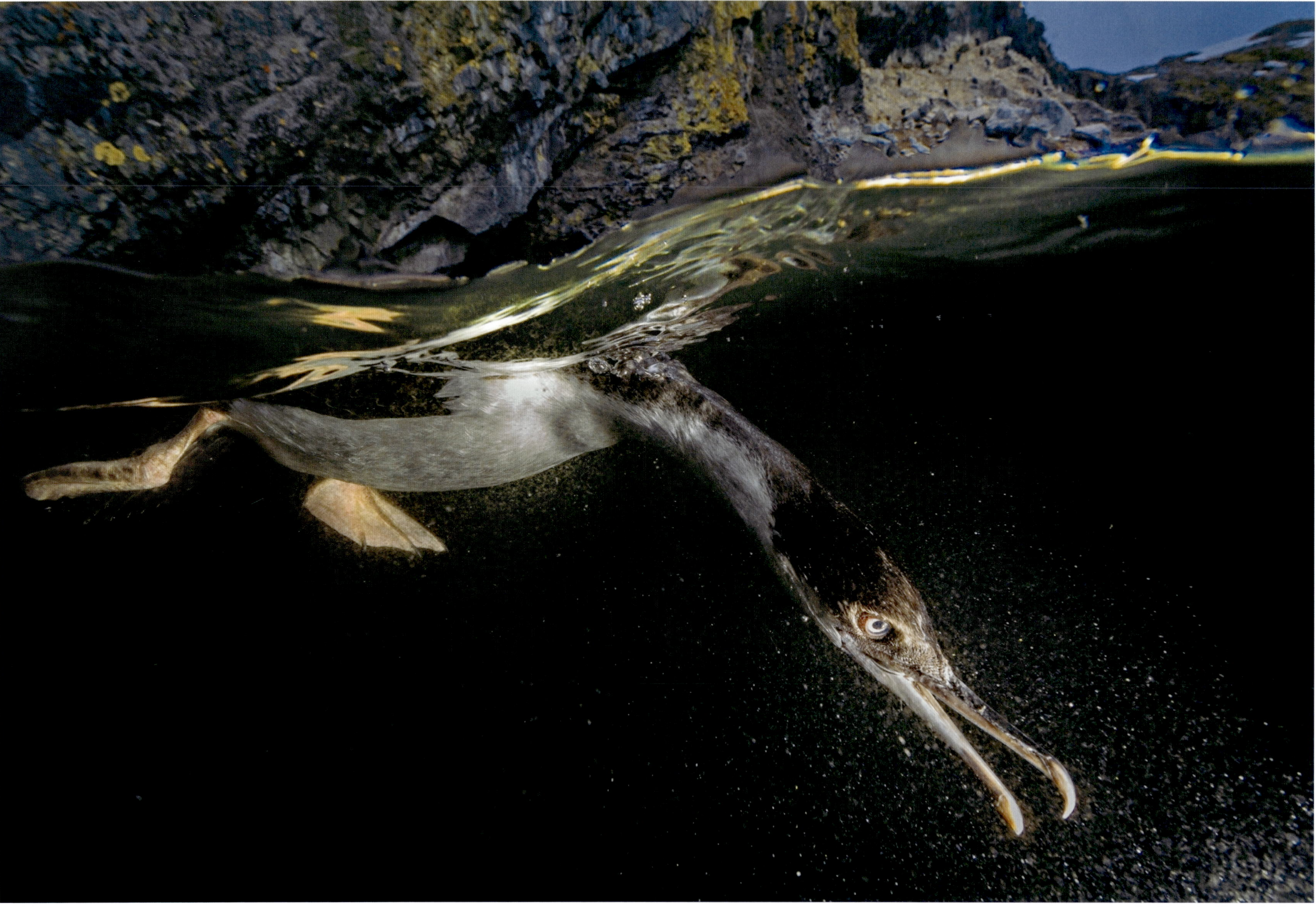

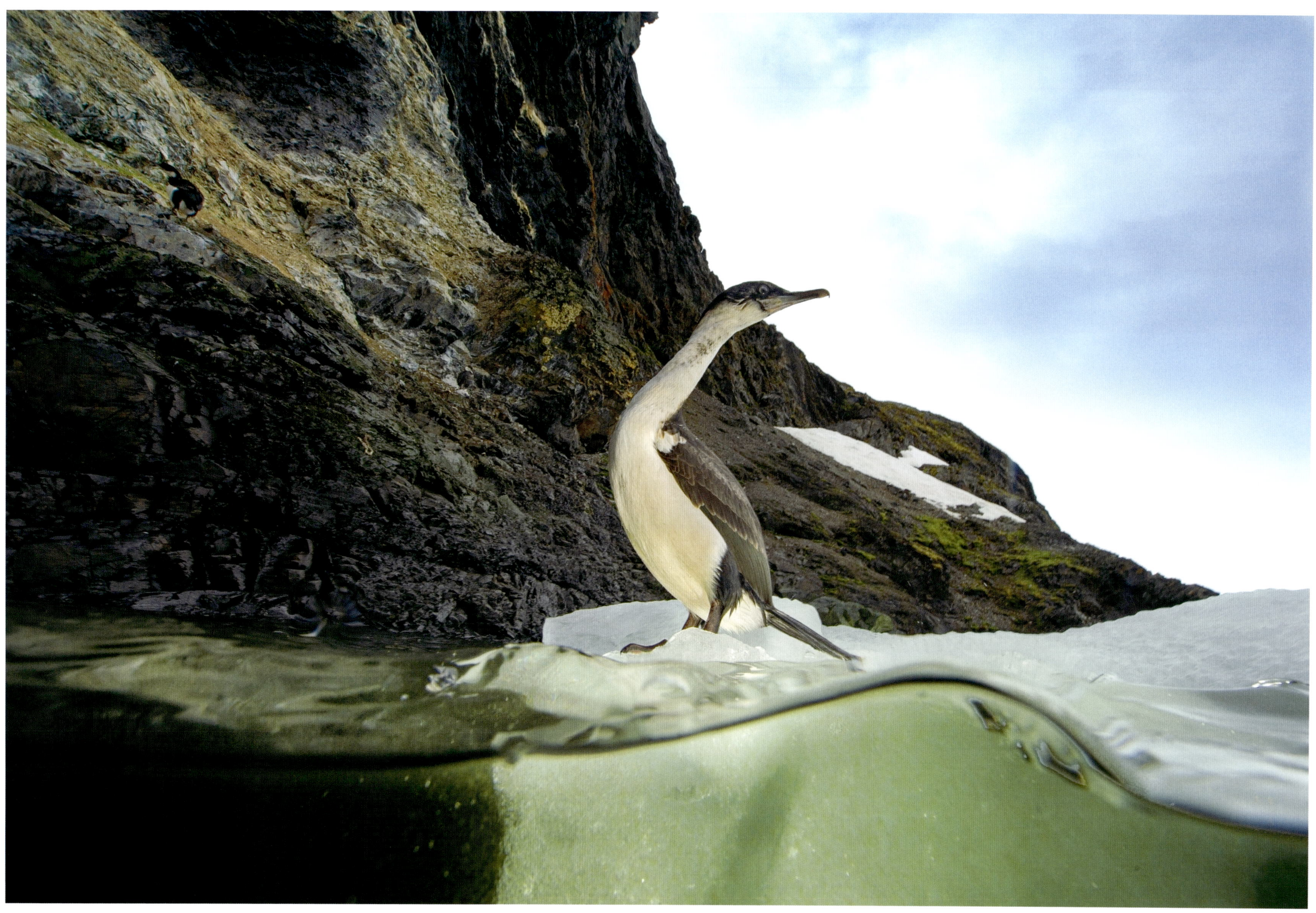

Southern Giant Petrel, Hercules Bay, South Georgia, 2016

A southern giant petrel (*Macronectes giganteus*) boldly glided up to my camera as I slowly swam toward a colony of macaroni penguins (*Eudyptes chrysolophus*) in Hercules Bay, South Georgia, in the sub-Antarctic. This sea-going scavenger – also known as the 'vulture of the southern oceans' – used its massive beak to taste-test my neoprene covered head. I was comfortable with the attention until it began to peck the glass dome on my housing. I made a few portraits and swam away, cuddling the camera protectively.

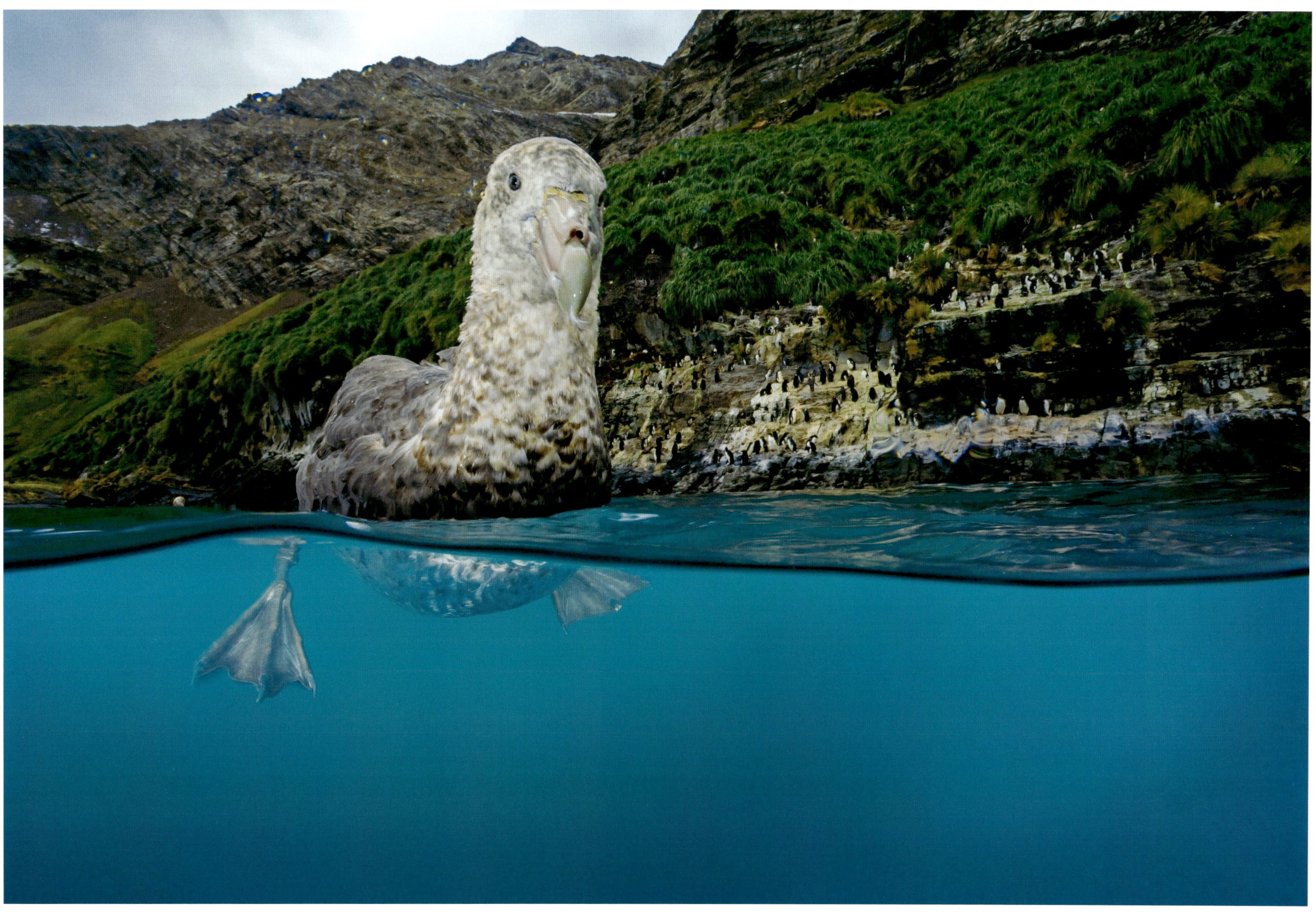

Stingrays and Clouds, Grand Cayman Island, 2015

Southern stingrays (*Hypanus americanus*) soar through a perfect studio
of sun-dappled sand, ultra-clear water and dramatic Caribbean sky.
When I first photographed here on a *National Geographic* assignment,
seven rays appeared each day for fishermen's scraps. With the story
came worldwide popularity and, more importantly, conservation. The now
protected population of rays has grown into a group of nearly 200 ocean
ambassadors, who greet thousands of tourist each day in one of the
most popular snorkel sites on the planet. As the sun sets and the last tour
boat leaves, the rays disappear back into their secret underwater lives.

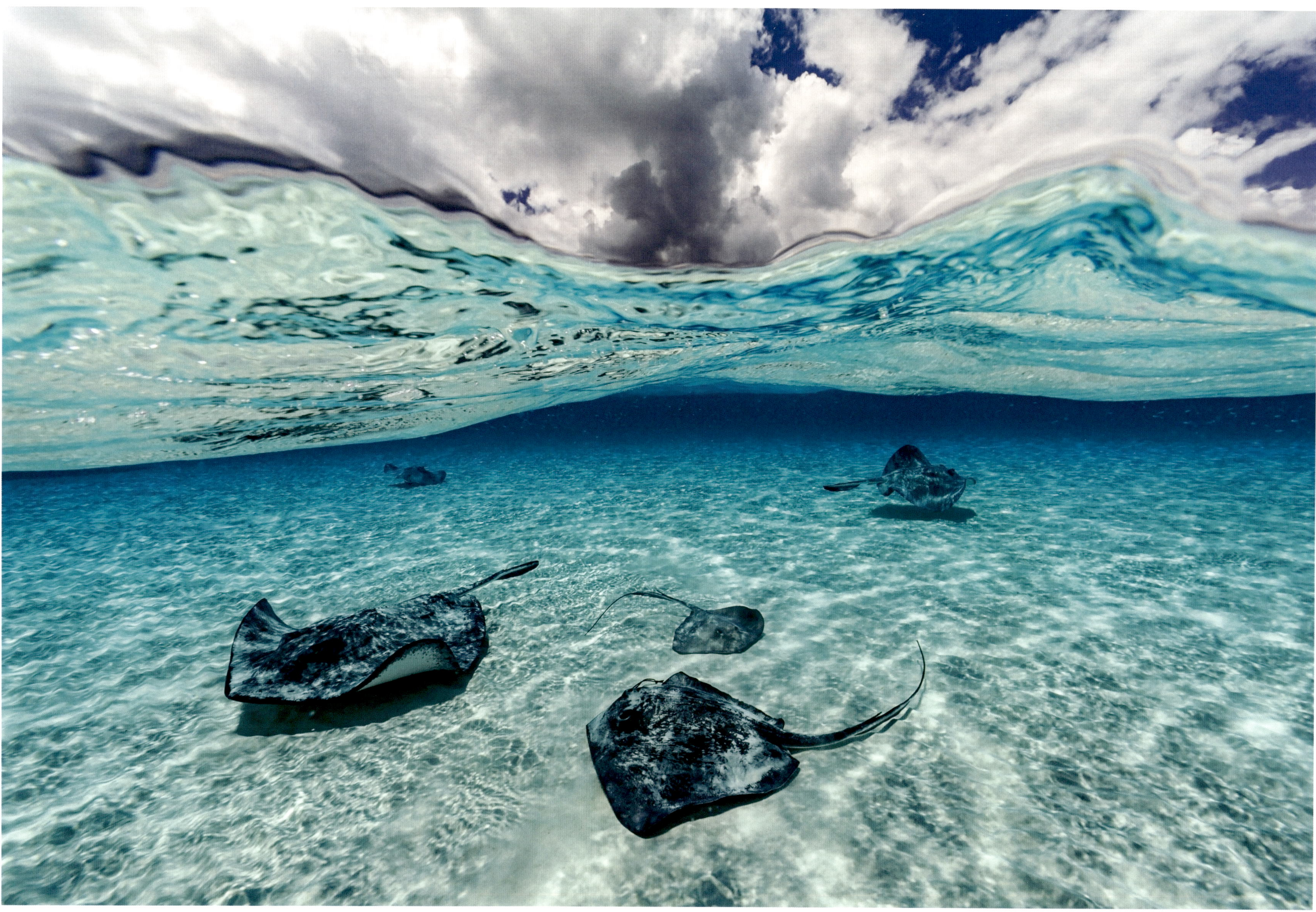

Stingray and Sailboat, North Sound, Grand Cayman Island, 1990

A solitary stingray glides through a stage of wave-raked sand, sea and
clouds in North Sound's shallows. All the elements came together in this
image, my first successful photographic merging of two worlds. As Kathy
Moran notes (page 6): 'The curve of the ray's wing mirrors the sweep of
the wave, while the chaos of the clouds creates a tension with the serenity
of the sand.'

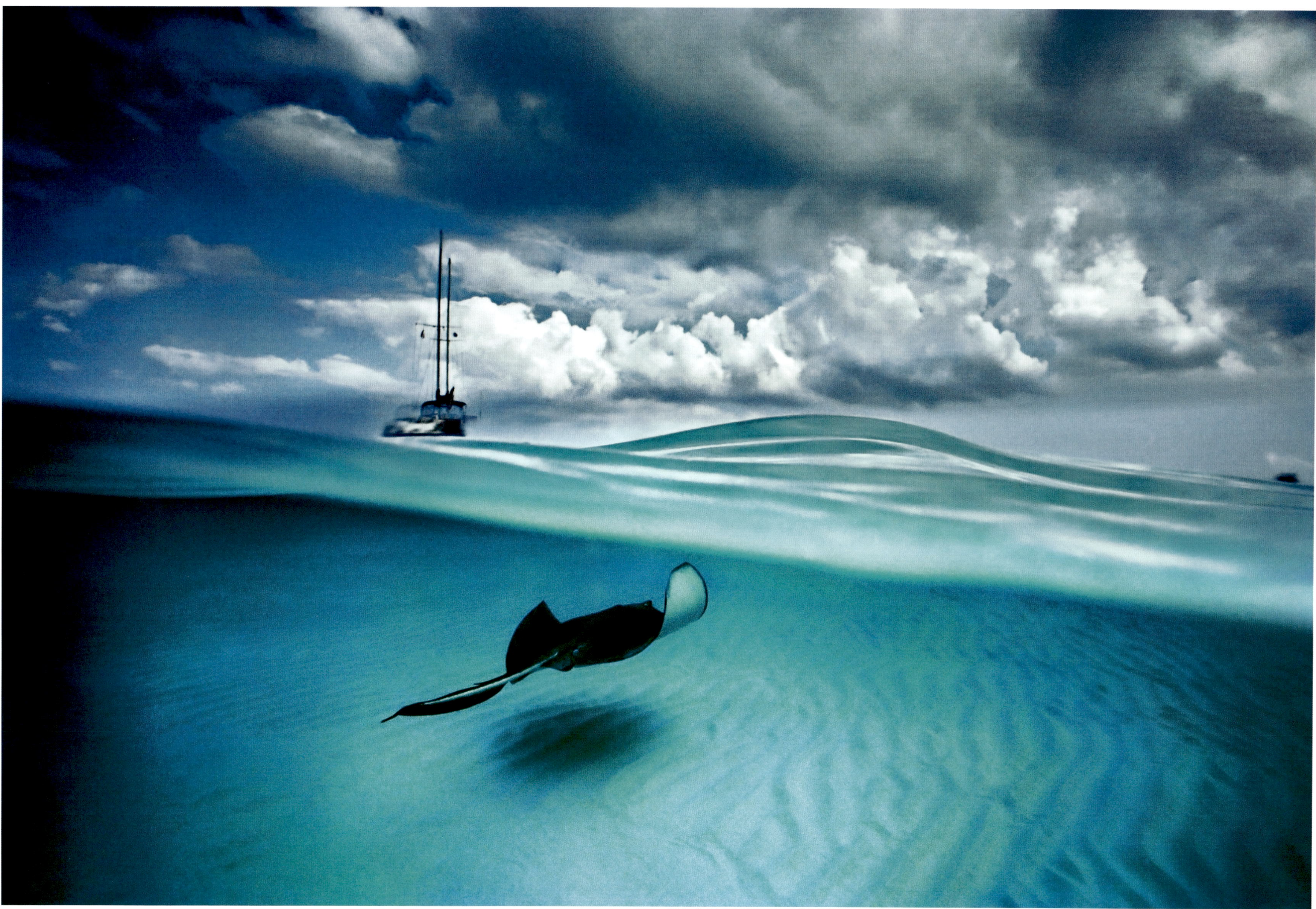

Bar Jacks, Grand Cayman Island, 1990

Bar jacks (*Caranx ruber*) stream across the shallow sand bar of
North Sound, where the combination of ultra-clear water and perfectly
wave-raked sand is a studio of dreams in the heart of the Caribbean.
There is a Zen-like simplicity here – a place of light, water and sky.

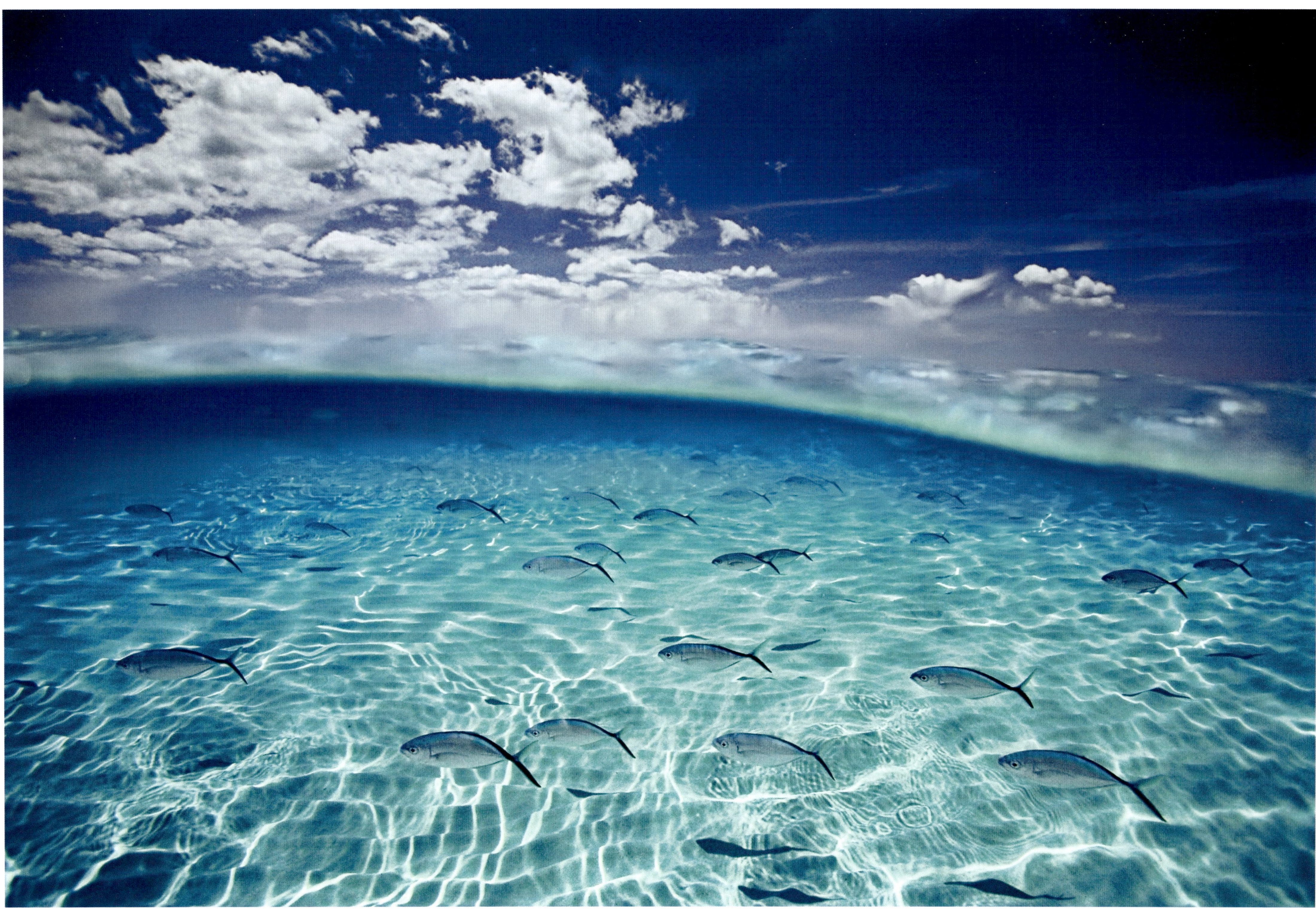

Elkhorn Coral Forest, Gardens of the Queen, Cuba, 2015

The setting sun casts a golden glow through the dense branches of
elkhorn coral (*Acropora palmata*). I saw my first Caribbean reef in 1958,
when I swam through forests of these corals bursting with dense schools
of fish. Now critically endangered, it has virtually vanished throughout
its original range but flourishes in the Gardens of the Queen, a protected
archipelago located 80 kilometres (50 miles) off the southern coast of
Cuba. Photographing here is like working inside a Caribbean museum,
where my memories are the reality.

American Crocodiles, Gardens of the Queen, Cuba, 2015
(overleaf, left and right)

Crocodiles have the ability to stop, hover, sink and rise like submarines.
Different species have different temperaments. American crocodiles
(*Crocodylus acutus*) in the Gardens of the Queen encounter snorkellers
and divers regularly. We work with caution here, but humans are
for the most part 'old hat' in their world. This is not the situation with
their aggressive cousins, the saltwater (*Crocodylus porosus*) and
Nile crocodiles (*Crocodylus niloticus*) which consider any encounter
a potential meal not to be missed. Scientists call these crocodiles
the 'engineers of the mangroves' because their movements open new
channels and increase circulation and productivity.

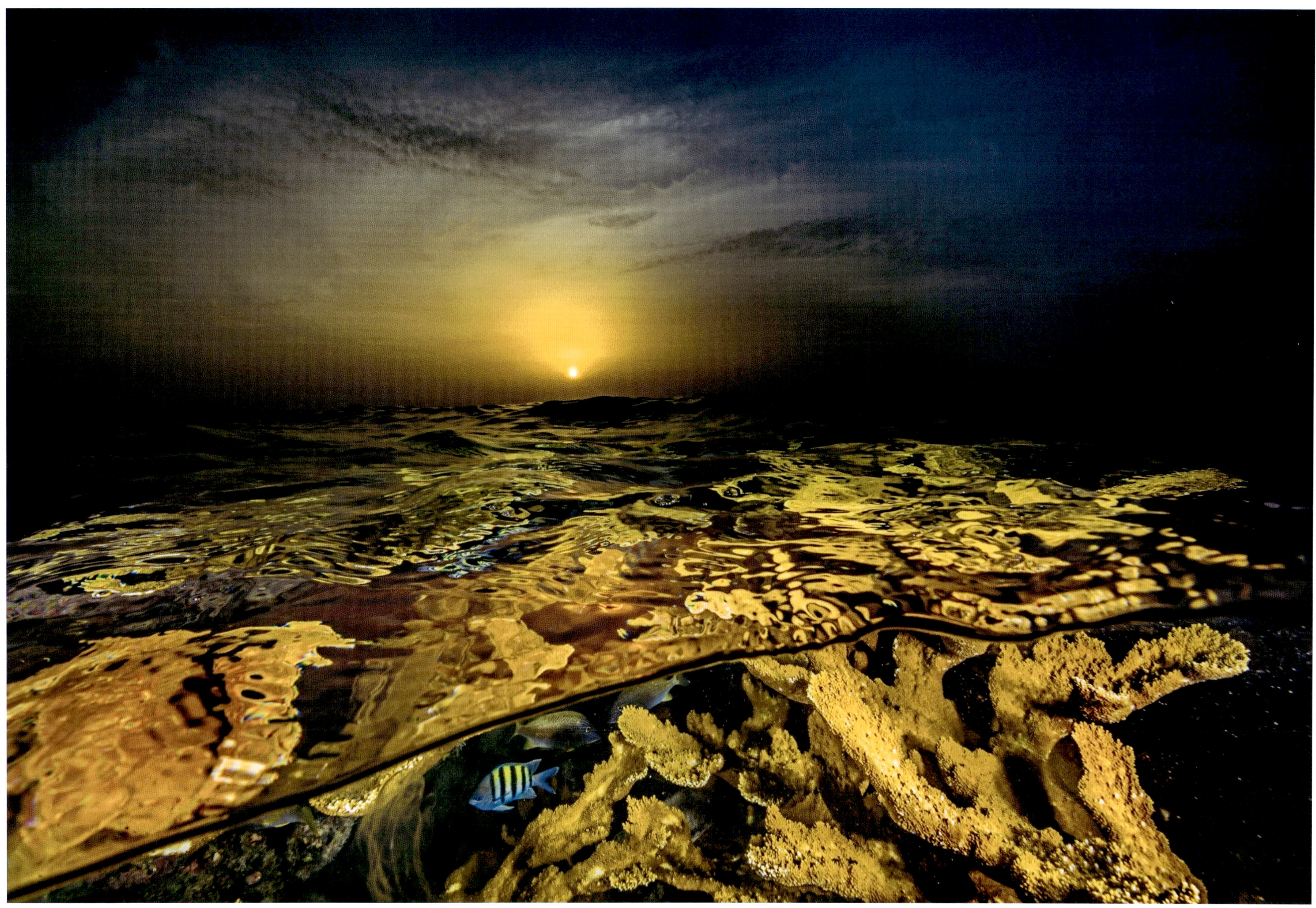

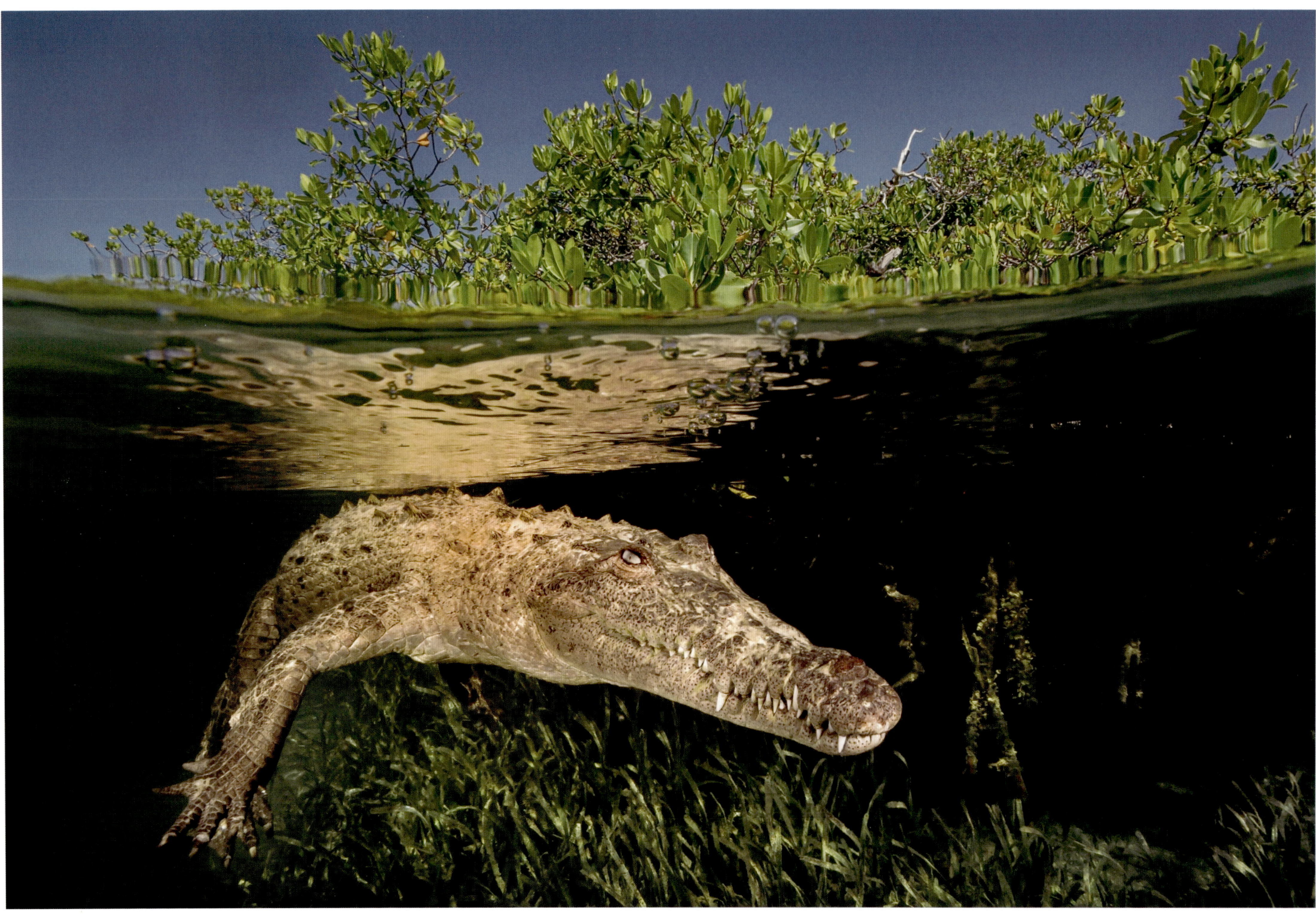

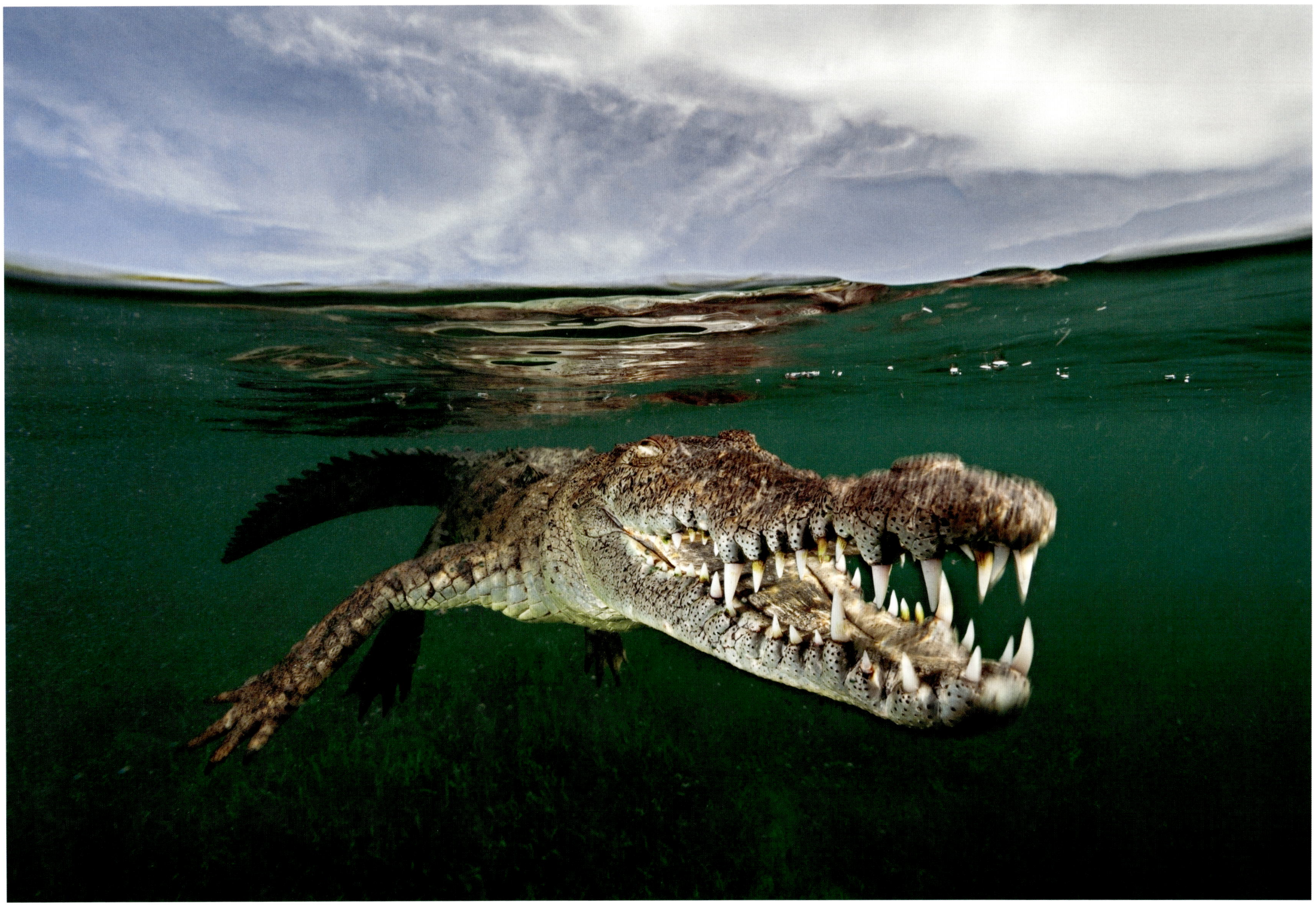

Hawksbill Hatchling, Gardens of the Queen, Cuba, 2015

This hawksbill sea turtle (*Eretmochelys imbricata*) hatchling was paddling furiously, heading for the safety of the open sea on the murky outgoing tide. It is very rare to encounter these creatures, which are smaller than the palm of your hand. The little turtle looked like it was swimming through a sea of stars beneath a painted sky. Remarkably, this corner of the Caribbean flourishes because of a combination of geographic isolation, geopolitics and vigilant patrols.

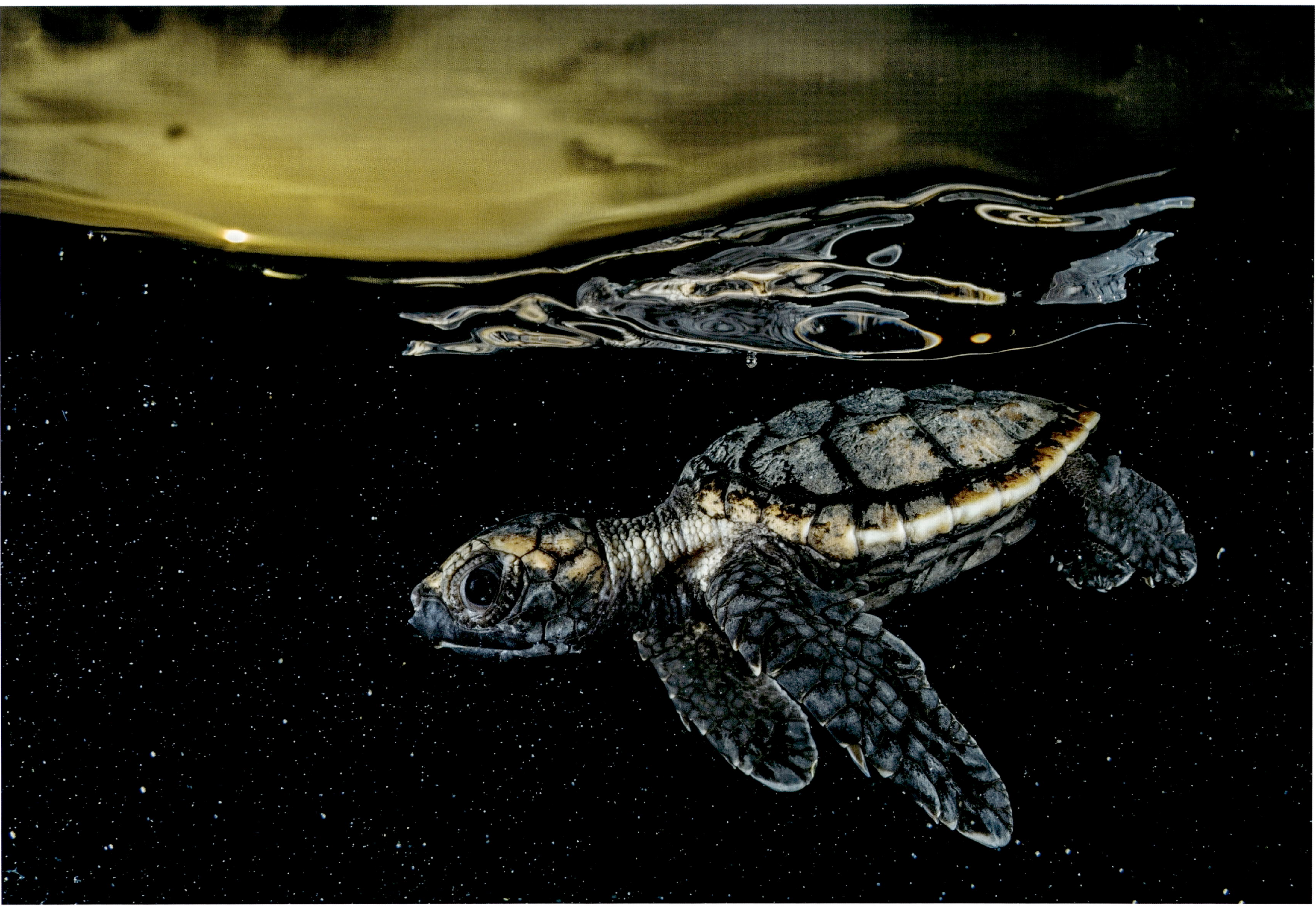

American Crocodile, Gardens of the Queen, Cuba, 2015

An American crocodile (*Crocodylus acutus*) glides in silence just beneath
the glass surface of the mangrove on a moonless night. The flash
strangely recorded the crocodile's wake, which perfectly mirrored its reptile
profile, including the curve of the eye. For a brief moment, I felt like
I was swimming eye-to-eye with a dinosaur.

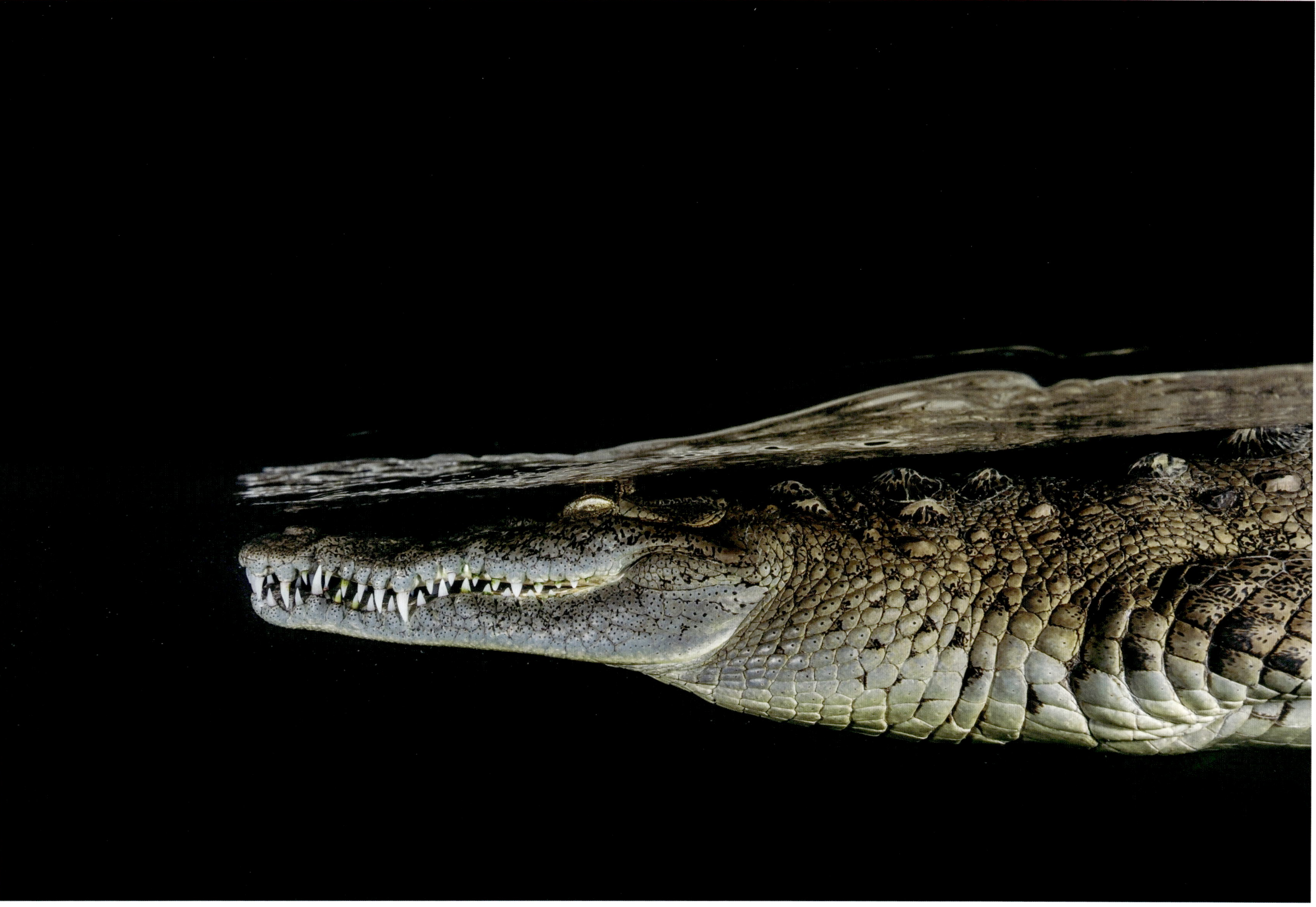

Silky Shark, Gardens of the Queen, Cuba, 2015

A silky shark (*Carcharhinus falciformis*) appears suspended between two worlds, a darkening sea below and a complicated Caribbean sky above. I like photographing as the day ends and the last light creates a shifting palette of dark greys, luminous whites and hints of purple. Silky sharks are pelagic predators (meaning they roam neither close to the bottom nor near the shore), patrolling the edge of the open ocean. They are named for their incredibly smooth skin that can reflect a camera's flash like moonlight.

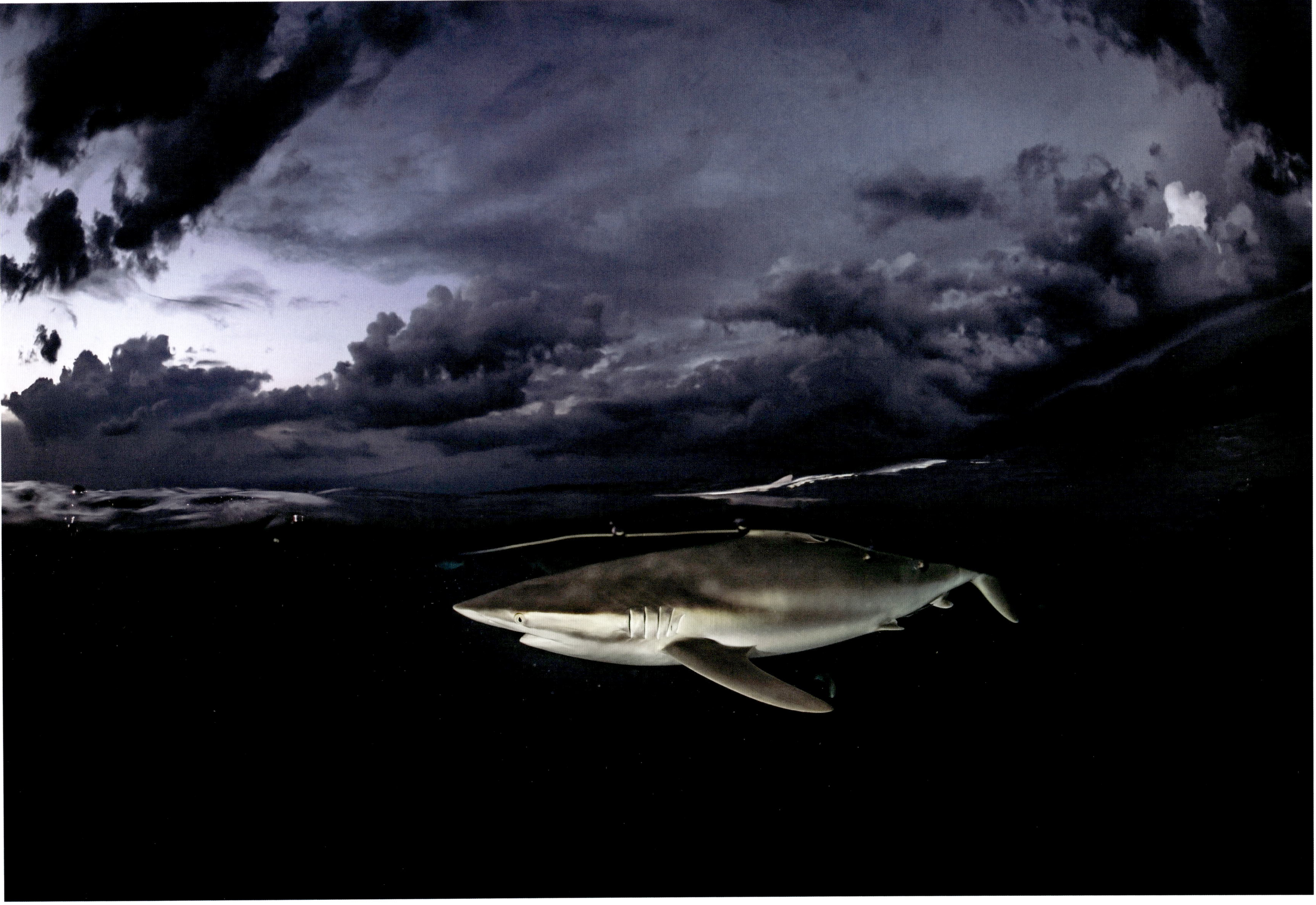

Lemon Shark, Bahama Banks, Commonwealth of the Bahamas, 2010

When I began diving, sharks were common, welcome encounters and
a sign of a healthy ecosystem, but they have since become ghosts in the
sea, overfished and absent from coral reefs and the open ocean. There
are places, fortunately, where their significance is celebrated and they are
protected. The Commonwealth of Bahamas recognized the economic
and environmental value of sharks with a ban on long lines in 1993,
followed by a declaration of shark sanctuary in 2011.

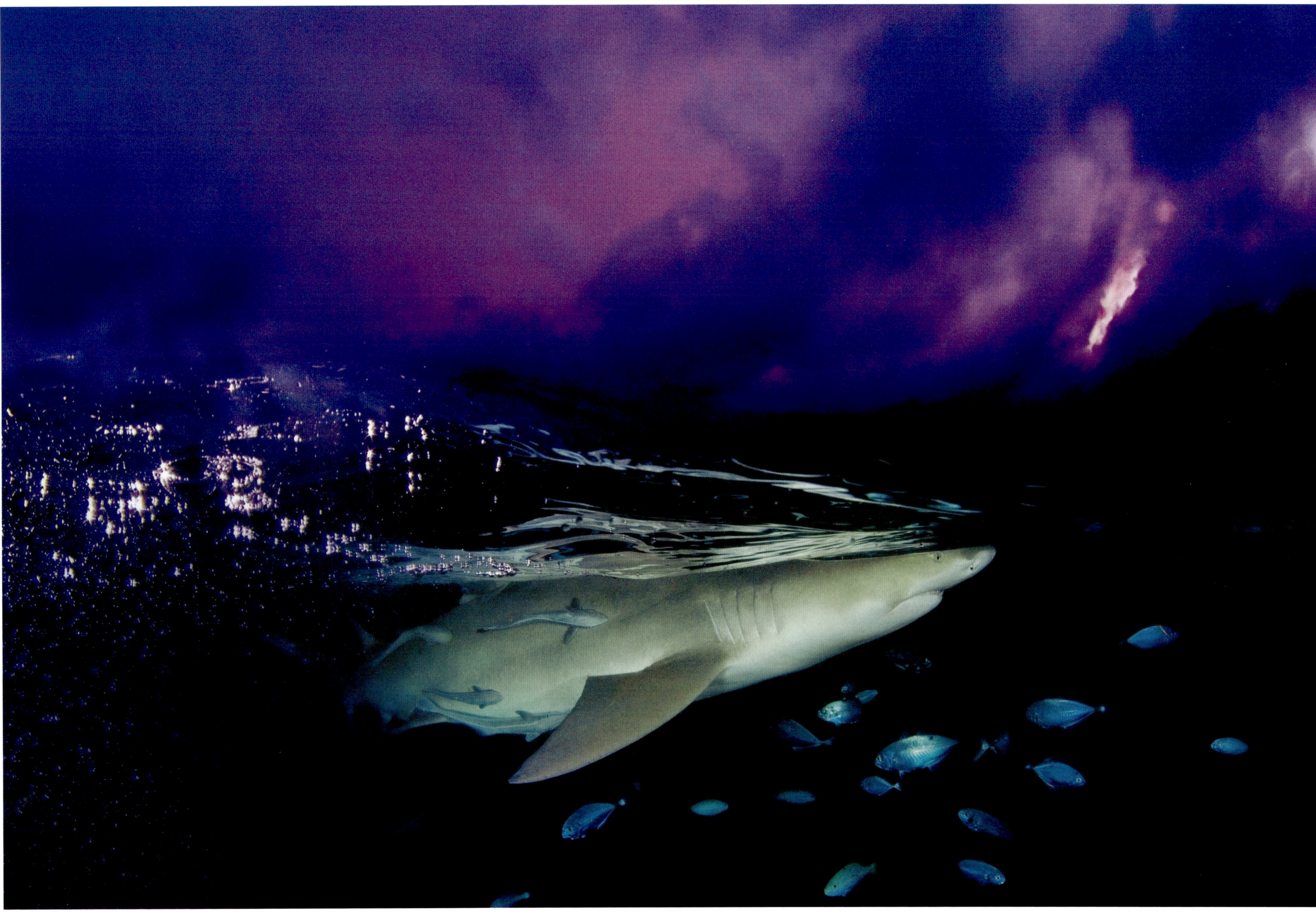

Lemon Sharks, Bahama Banks, Commonwealth of the Bahamas, 2010

I went into the water just after sunset to photograph lemon sharks
(*Negaprion brevirostris*). The surface of the sea always produces
a constant surprise. Here, a rapid blink of the strobe turned a wave
into crystal, revealing a squadron on patrol beneath a luminous sky.

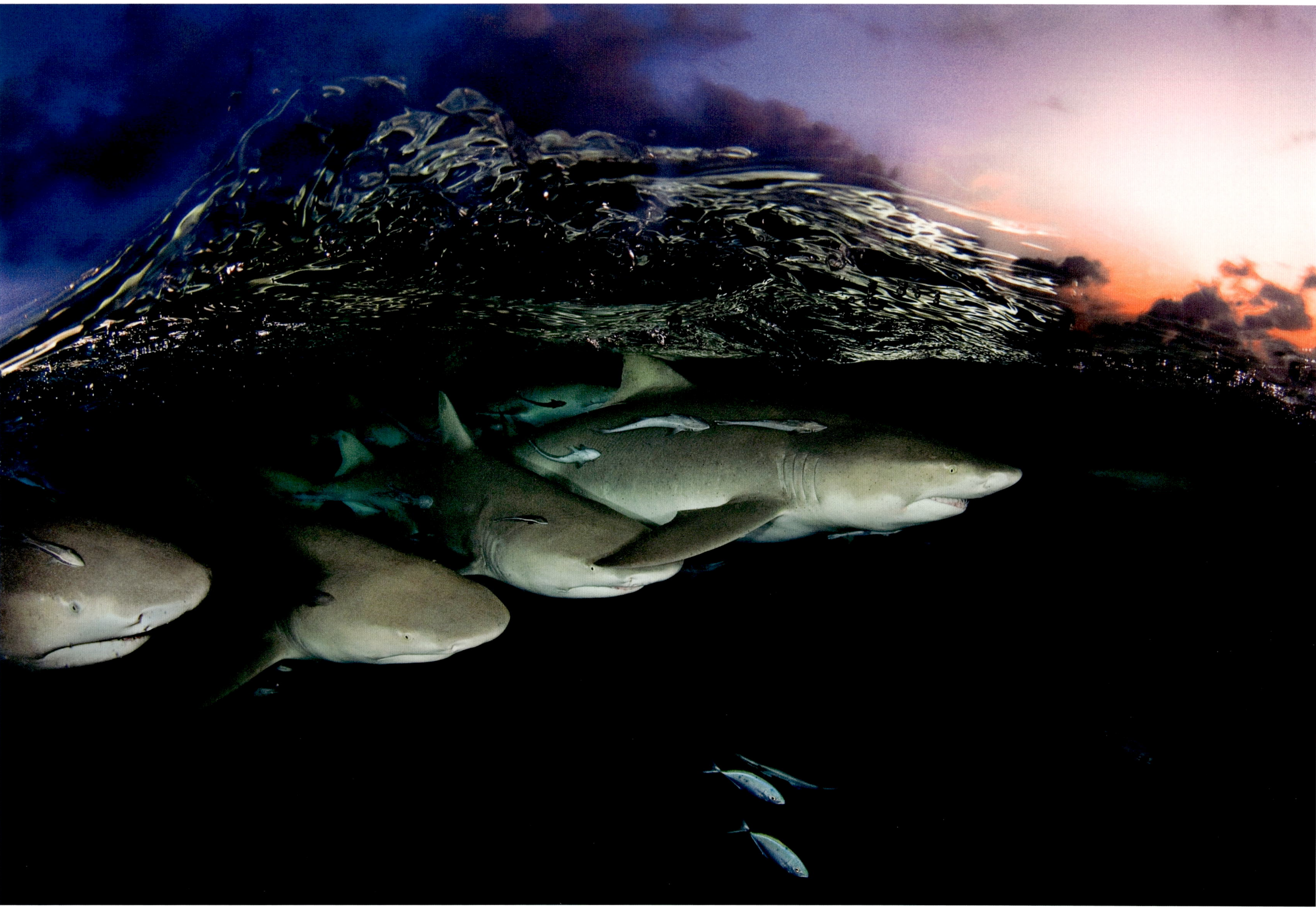

Sargassum, Yucatan Peninsula, Mexico, 2018

Sargassum is a living seaweed ceiling on the sea; it knows no borders
and has neither fixed location nor coordinates. This golden canopy, named
by the Portuguese, is a habitat for schools of fish that are both predator
and prey. During recent explosive growth related to climate change,
endless sargassum mats have drifted westward across the Caribbean,
attracting marine life like the plains of Africa attract nomadic herbivores.
When the blooming rafts of weed accumulate on Yucatan shores, they
smother beaches causing environmental and economic damage.

Sargasso Sea, Bermuda, 2013 (overleaf, left)

Forests of sargassum seaweed appear and disappear at the will of wind
and wave in the Sargasso Sea surrounding Bermuda. This unique sea
does not have a coastline and takes its name from the seaweed that
concentrates into oceanic gardens flooded with light and unexpected
life. The world of seaweed can be as small as a softball or miles wide,
but no matter the size, creatures will be toiling to survive in this universe
of tangled branches.

Sea Turtle Sanctuary, Florida, USA, 2014 (overleaf, right)

A loggerhead turtle hatchling (*Caretta caretta*) hides in the golden
branches of sargassum in the Gulf Stream, off the coast of Florida.
The floating forest is a critical nursery for these vulnerable reptiles,
which are on every predators' menu.

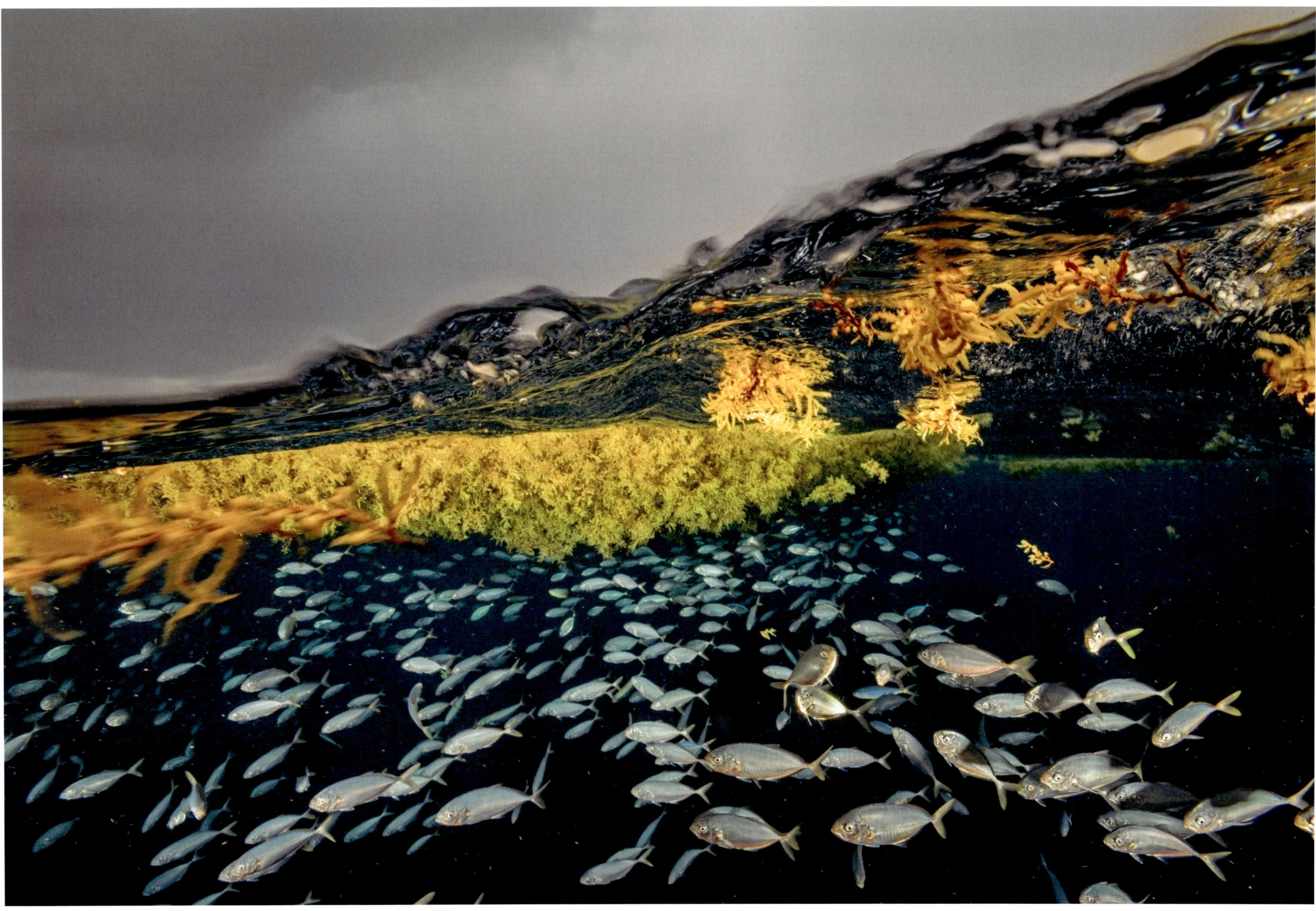

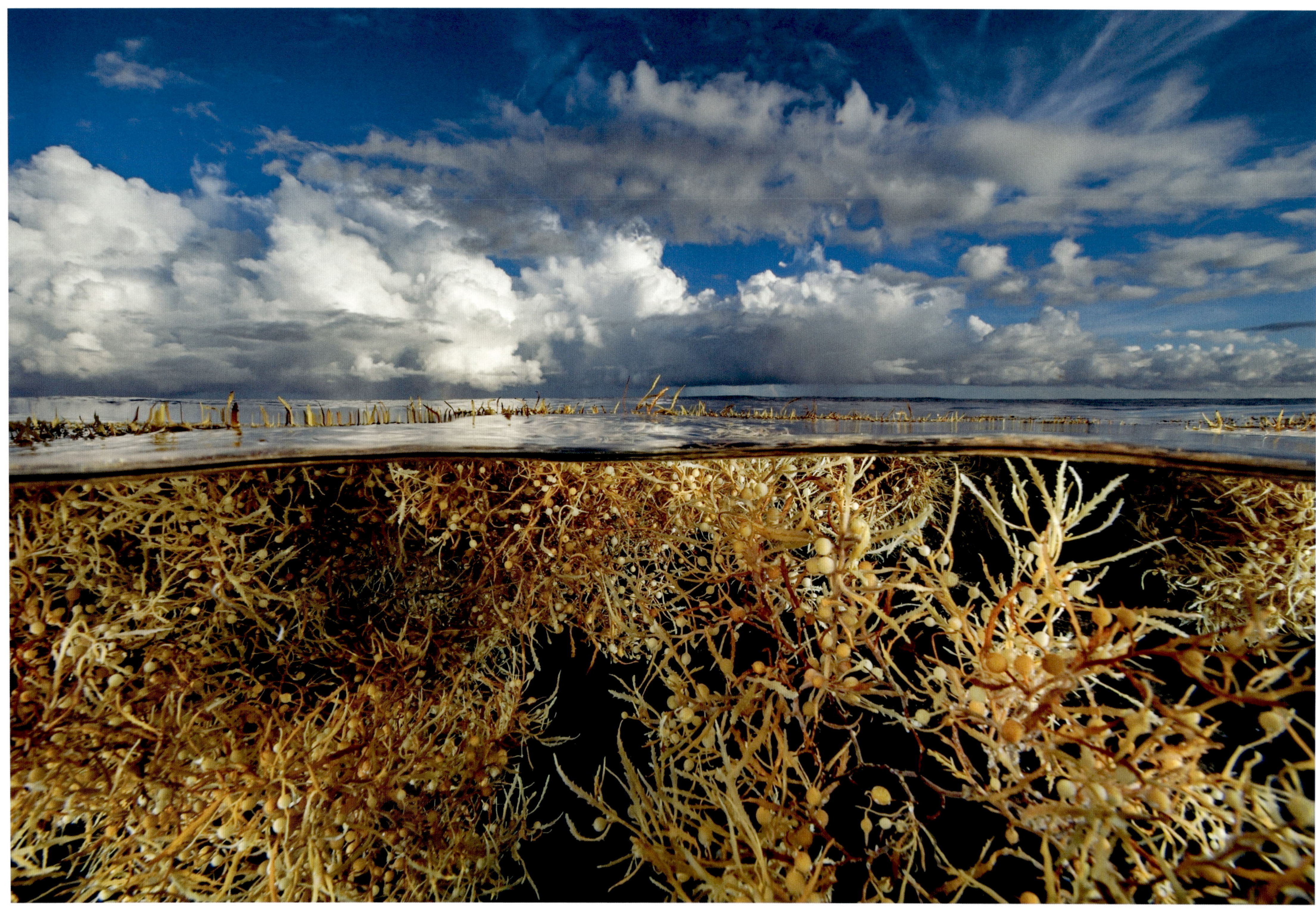

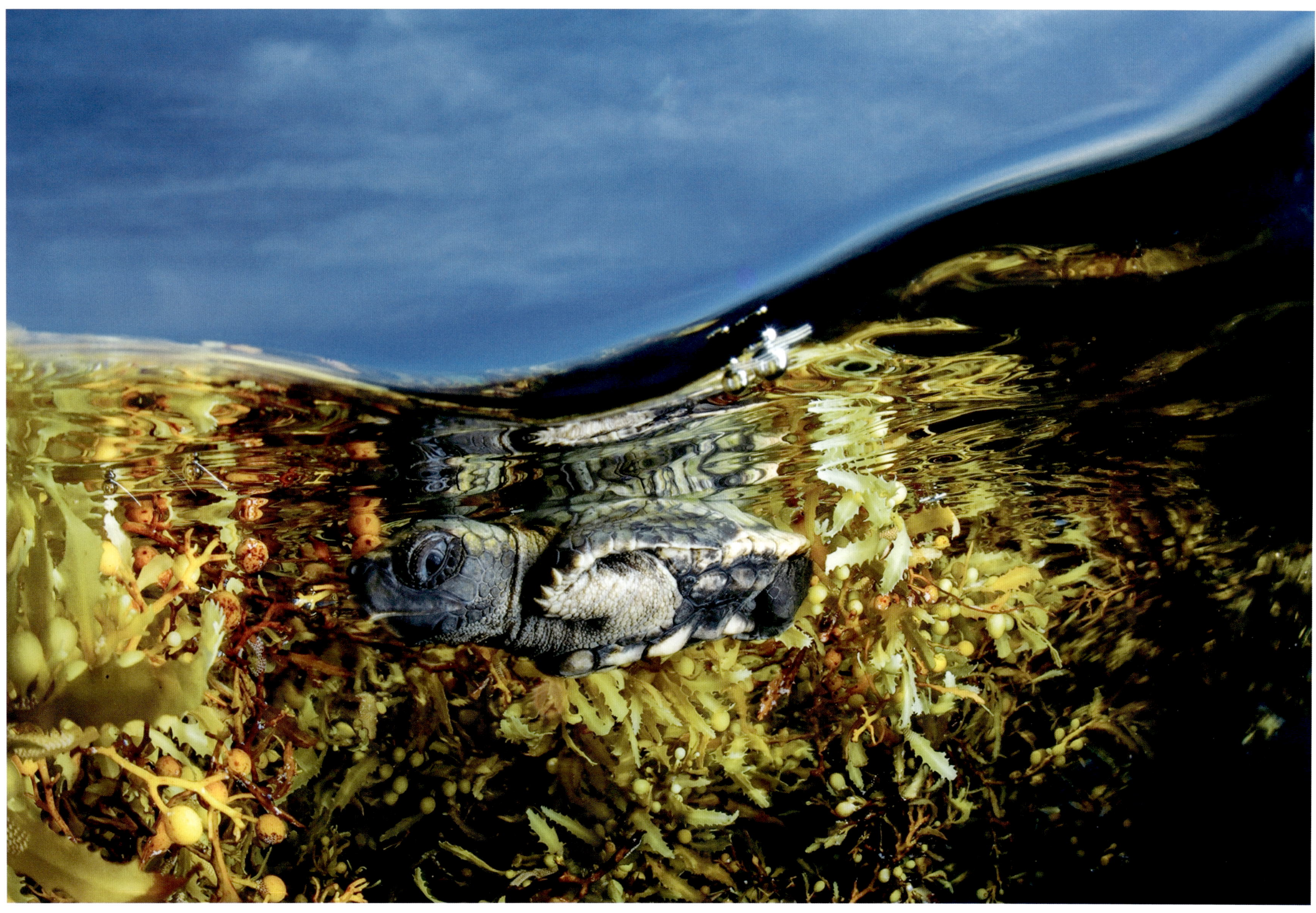

Grey Triggerfish, Sargasso Sea, Bermuda, 2013

Floating debris in the sea has become a found habitat for many creatures,
including these grey triggerfish (*Balistes capriscus*). The remains of
this plastic crate were the site of continuous battles for ownership and
occupancy. Ocean gyres concentrate sargassum weed and marine debris
on an endless carousel of currents that form the Sargasso Sea. As I
worked here, I recalled centuries-old lore of ships lost and doomed to an
eternity in the gyres of the Bermuda Triangle.

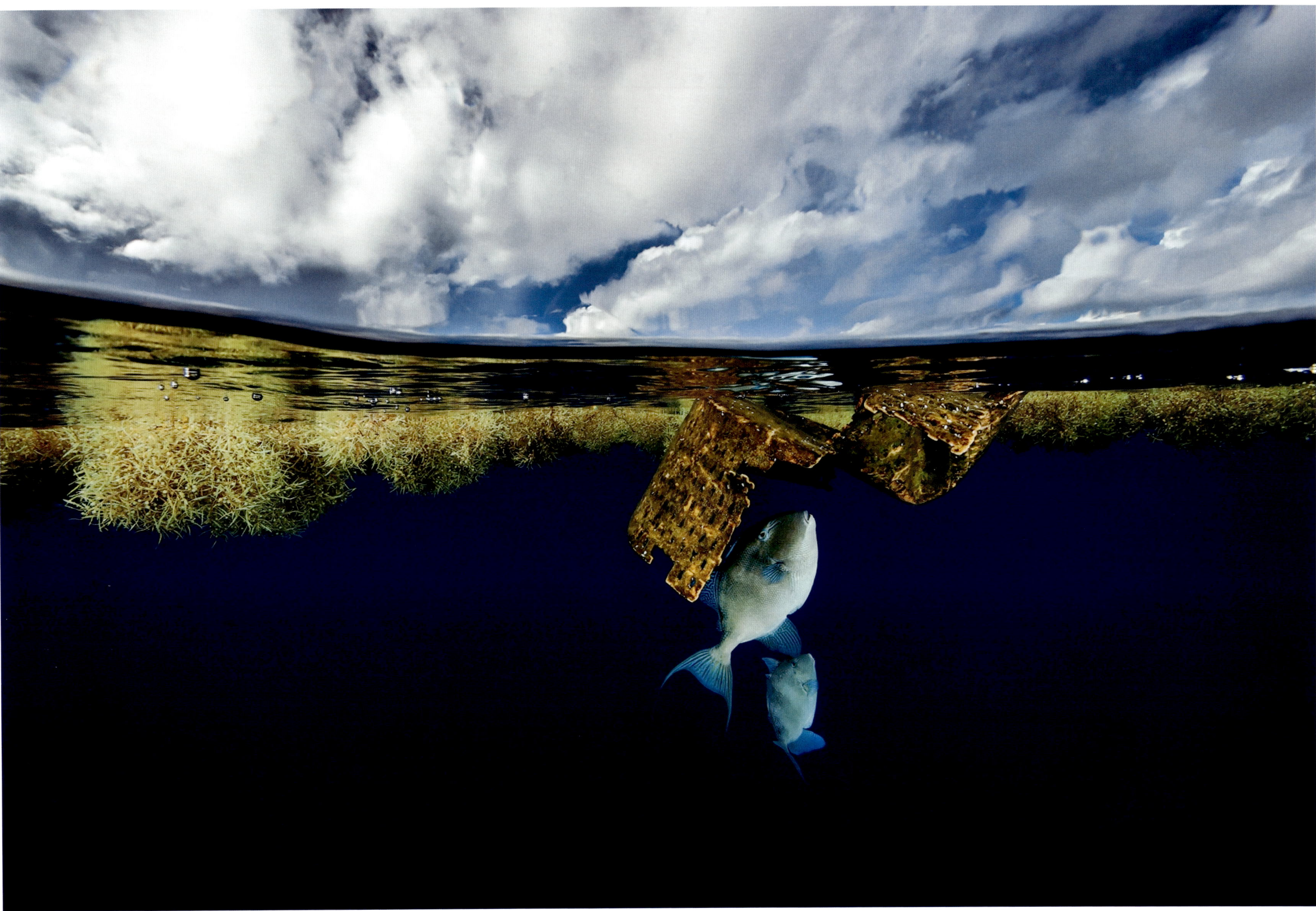

Nxamasere Channel, Okavango Delta, Botswana, 2003

The Okavango River is born from the rains in the mountains of Angola and
flows into Botswana, forming a vast delta (a UNESCO World Heritage
Site) that from space looks like a hand over the Kalahari Desert. It is
a river system that never makes its way to the sea. During a dive, I heard
the sound of singing and looked up through a tangle of lilies to see a man
effortlessly balanced in his narrow *mokoro* (canoe), gliding toward me
under an impossibly blue sky. He stopped singing when he saw me,
but there remained the rhythmic sound of the wooden *ngashi* (pole) as
he pushed himself downstream. The deep channels in this region are
a system of braided boulevards used by humans and wildlife alike.

Floodwater, Okavango Delta, Botswana, 2003 (overleaf, left)

The floodwaters arrive in the mid-delta bringing life to the floodplains.
Recent seasons have delivered less water and caused extreme drought
conditions in the southwestern regions of the delta, threatening this
miracle of life.

Africa's Secret Gardens, Okavango Delta, Botswana, 2003
(overleaf, right)

Lily gardens grow beneath the papyrus-lined channels of the Panhandle
region of the Okavango Delta. Working below the surface here is like
photographing inside a Monet painting, except you never know if a Nile
crocodile or hippo will appear.

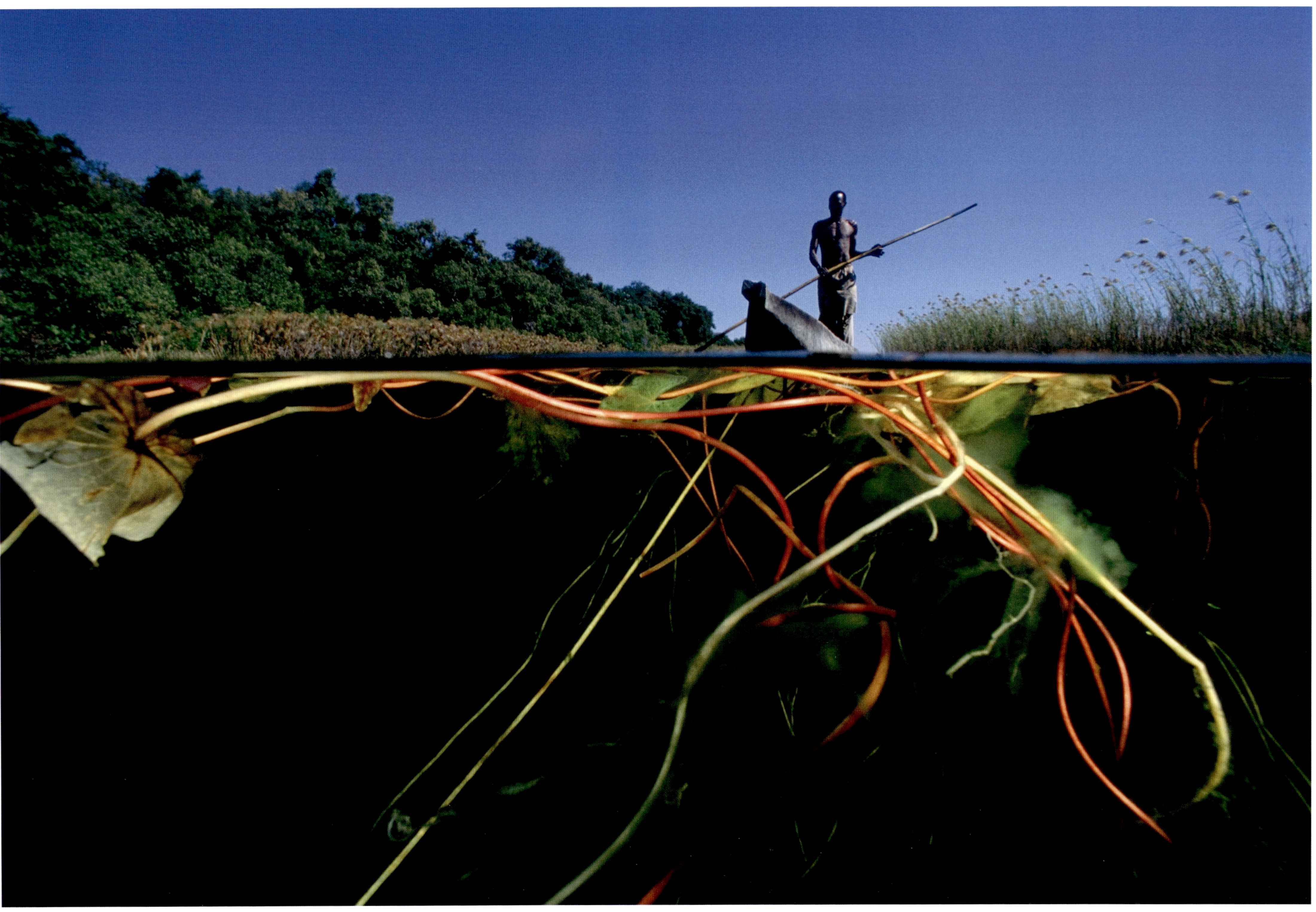

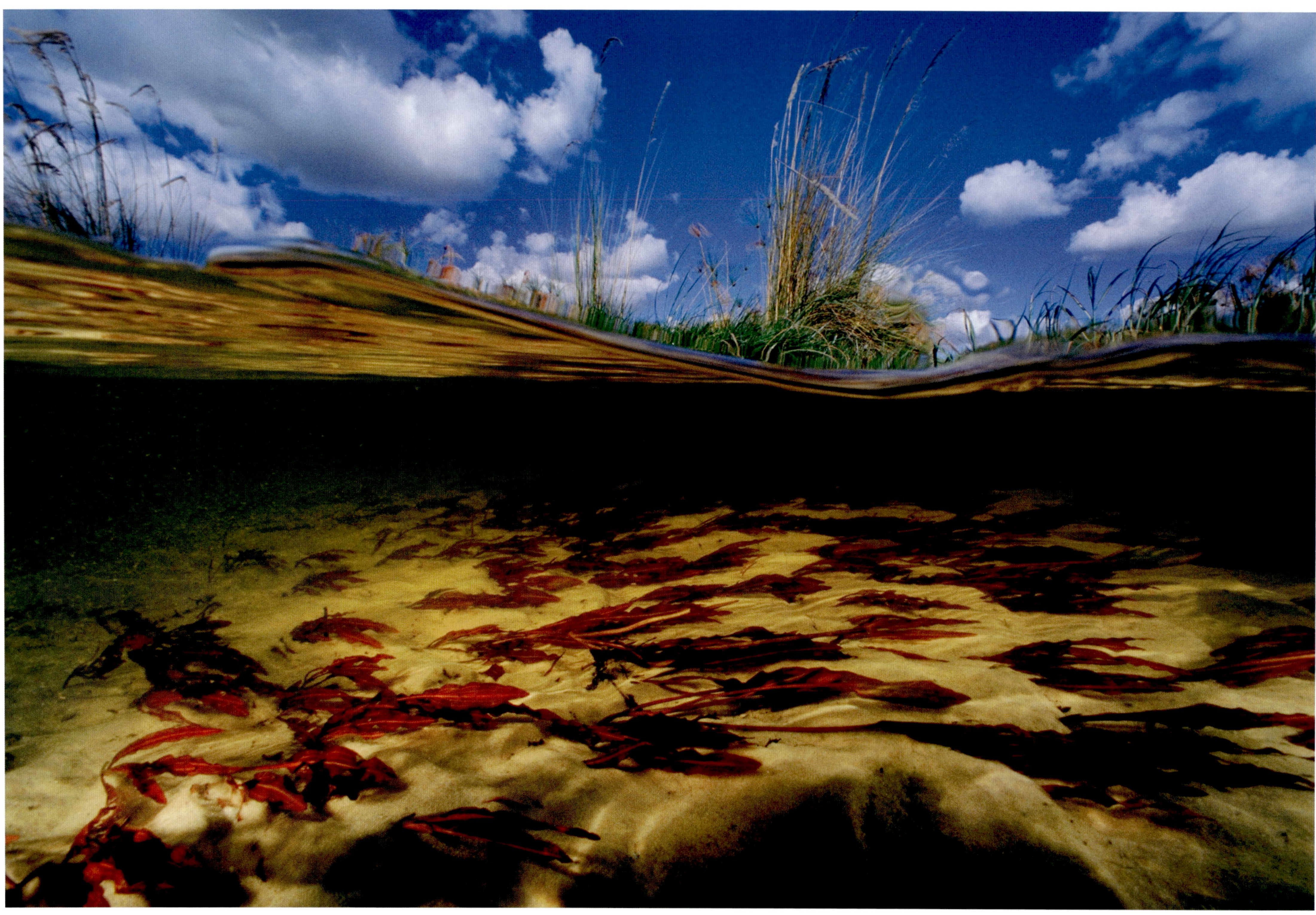

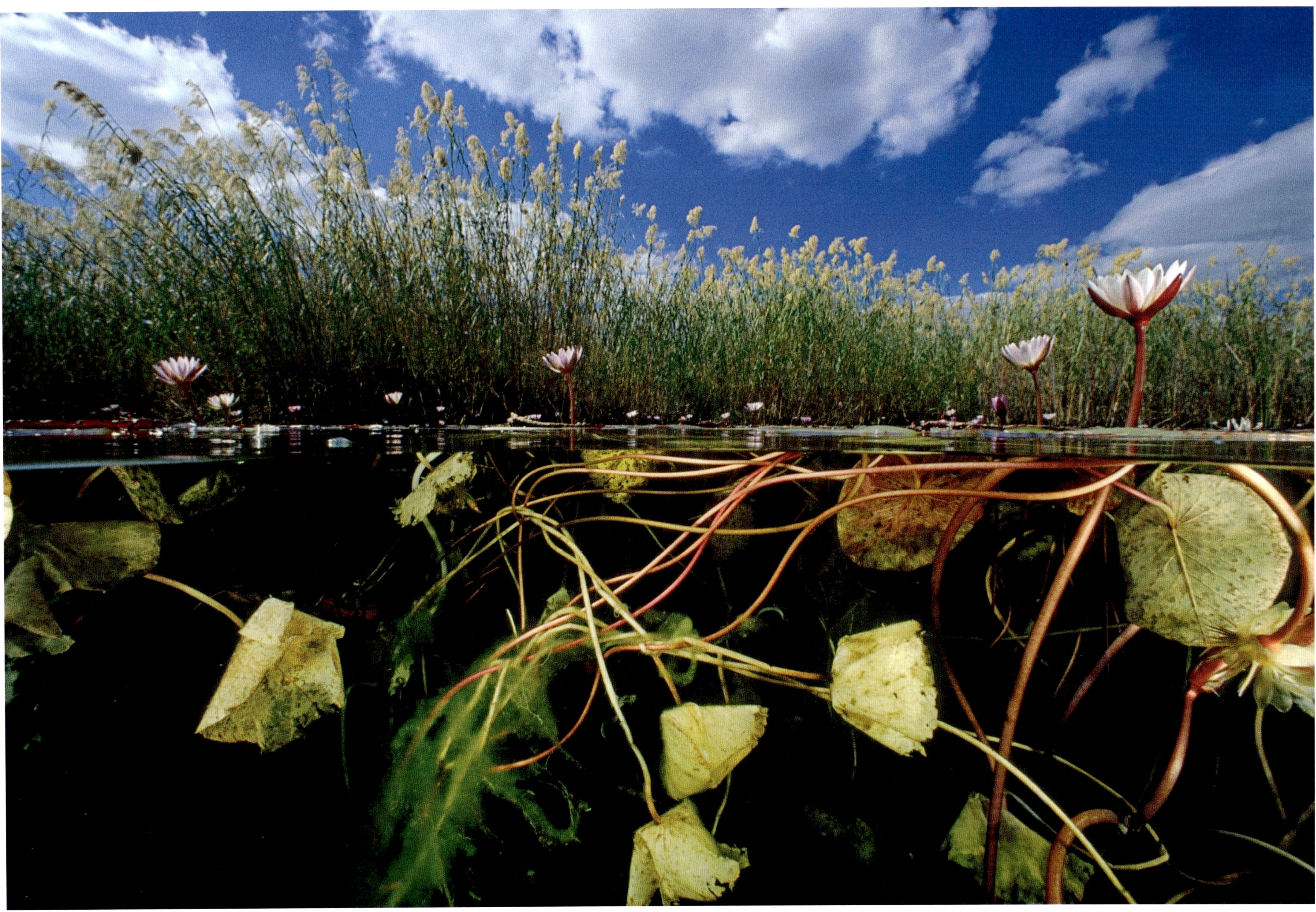

A purple lion's mane jellyfish (*Cyanea capillata*) – one of the largest jellyfish
species – pulses through emerald waters that mimic the colours of the
evergreen forest above in Bonne Bay Fjord, Gros Morne National Park. The
cold depths of the nearly isolated fjord allow arctic marine life to survive
next to the slightly warmer waters of the Gulf of St Lawrence.

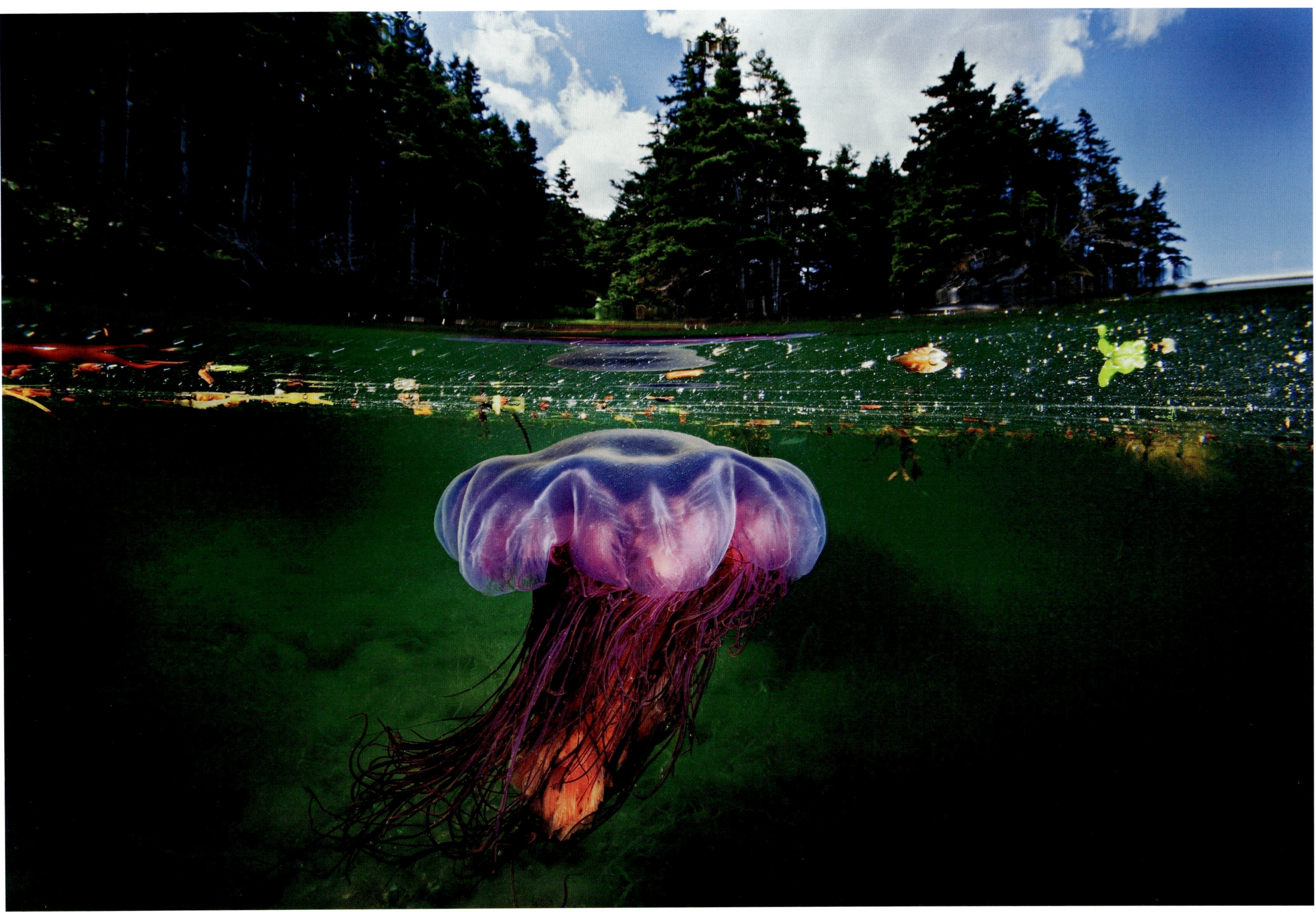

Western Brook Pond, Gros Morne National Park, Newfoundland, Canada, 2012

Massive cliffs towered 600 metres (2,000 feet) above us as we descended into one of the most pristine freshwater vaults on the planet to explore glacially sculpted rocks from the basement of time in Western Brook Pond. Cut off from the sea, this 165-metre-deep (541-foot) fjord is a starkly beautiful geological museum in Gros Morne National Park. It is a UNESCO World Heritage Site formed millions of years ago by colliding ice-age landmasses and grinding glaciers.

Midnight Capelin, Labrador, Canada, 2012 (overleaf, left)

Thousands of capelin (*Mallotus villosus*) select a narrow section of sand beach in L'Anse-au-Loup upon which to spawn. It is a chaotic pulse of life in six inches of water beneath crystalline waves in the dark Labrador night.

Herring Trap, Raleigh, Newfoundland, Canada, 2012 (overleaf, right)

A herring trap is a traditional fishing method. As the dory crew hauled the herring trap to their boat, I was surrounded by a hurricane of silver desperation as the school began to swim furiously toward the edges of the net. John Taylor and his crew are a vanishing breed; he dreams of another way of life for his son.

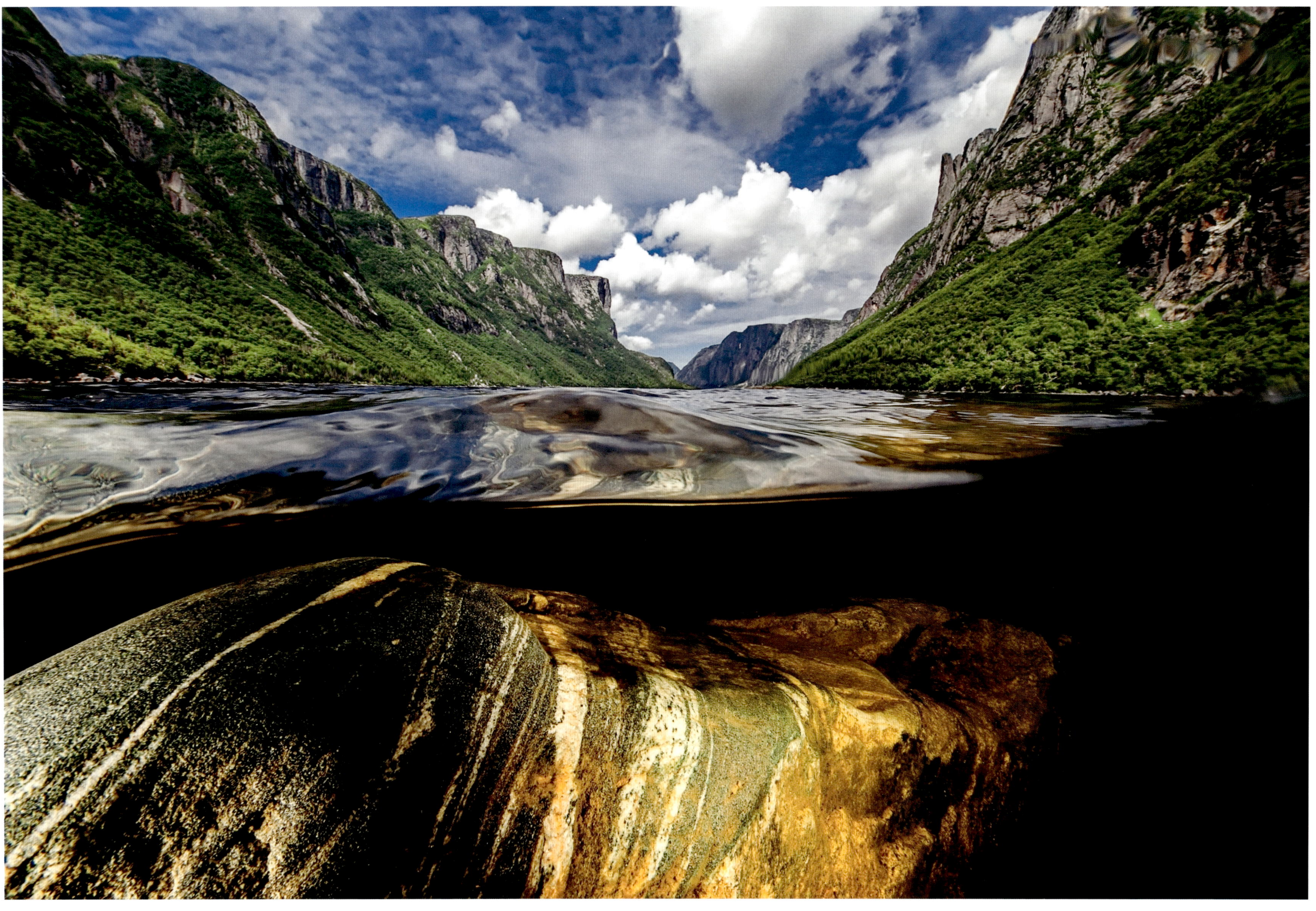

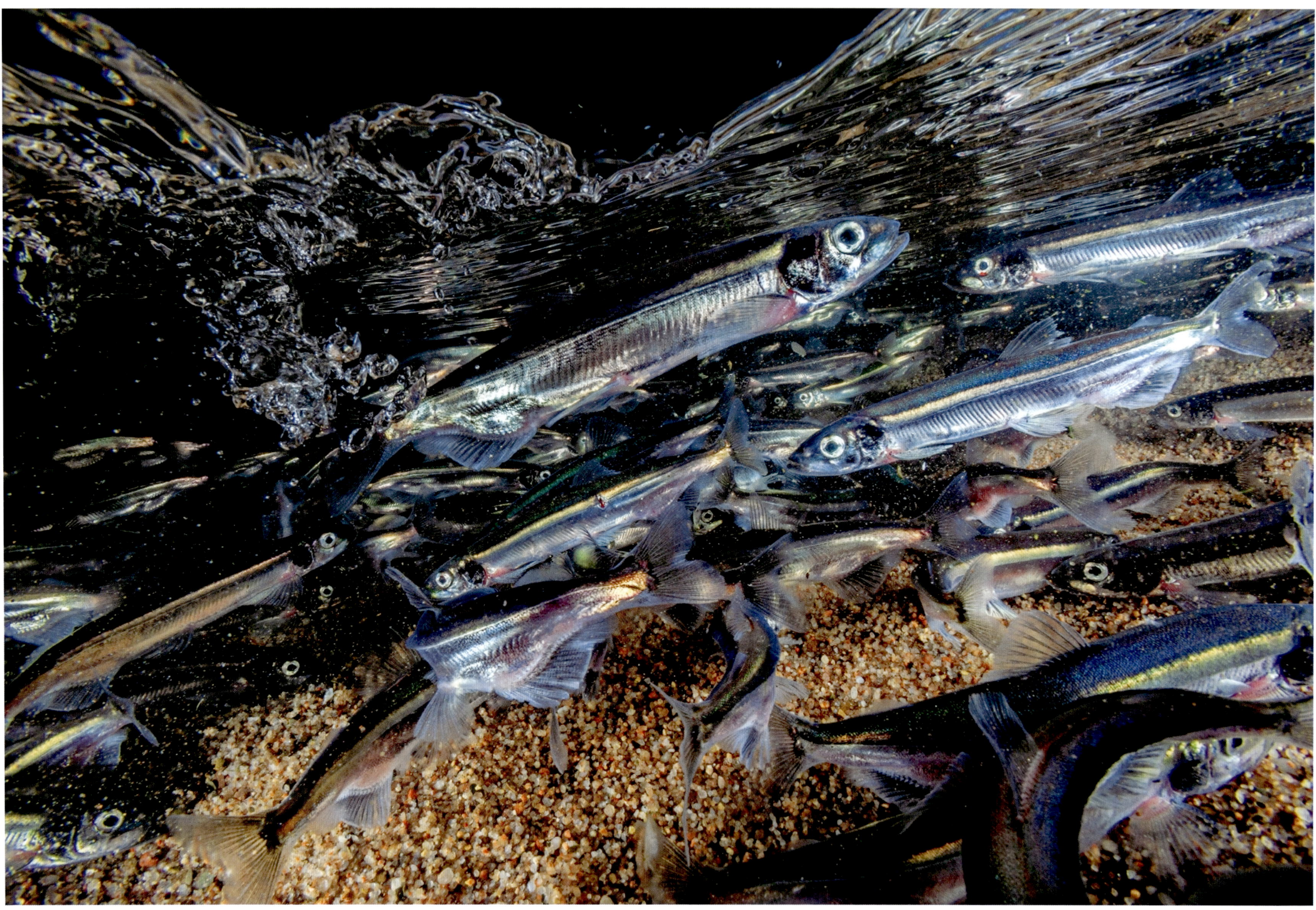

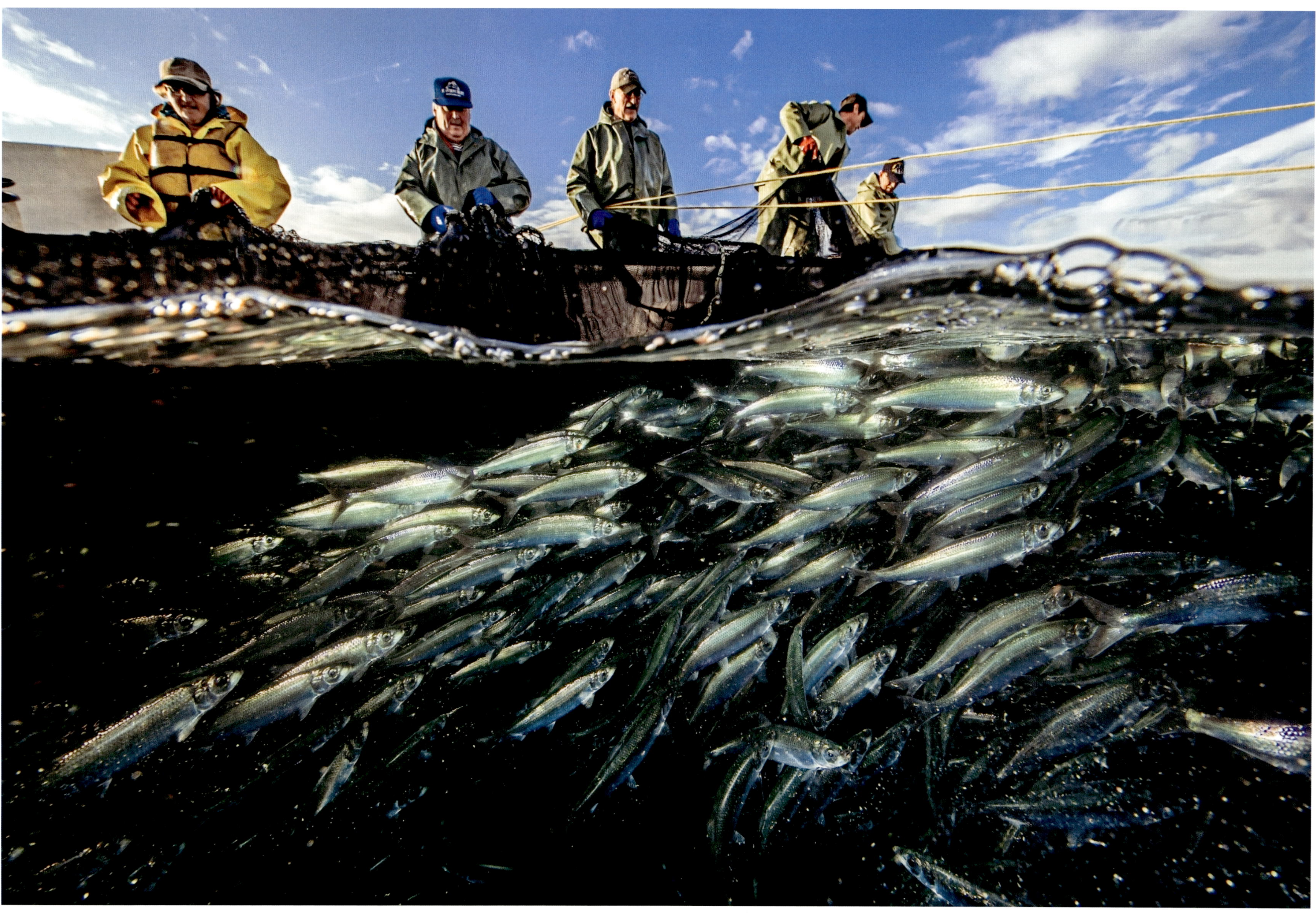

Harp Seal Pup, Gulf of St Lawrence, Canada, 2011

Sometimes an assignment changes your life: you start a story that you
never leave, and it never leaves you. The Gulf of St Lawrence is one such
story. Harp seals (*Pagophilus groenlandicus*) are born on the sea ice near
Magdalen Island in the centre of the Gulf of St Lawrence. They are born
with yellow-tinged coats that will turn brilliant white, making them some of
the world's most beautiful creatures, with their cloud-soft fur and obsidian
eyes. This 'white coat' waits patiently for its mother to return. The pups
are nursed for 12 to 15 days before the mother abandons them to mate
with nearby males and then migrate back to Arctic waters. Pups require
a few weeks of stable ice to grow and mature. As temperatures rise,
the sea ice nursery shrinks or disintegrates causing catastrophic loss.

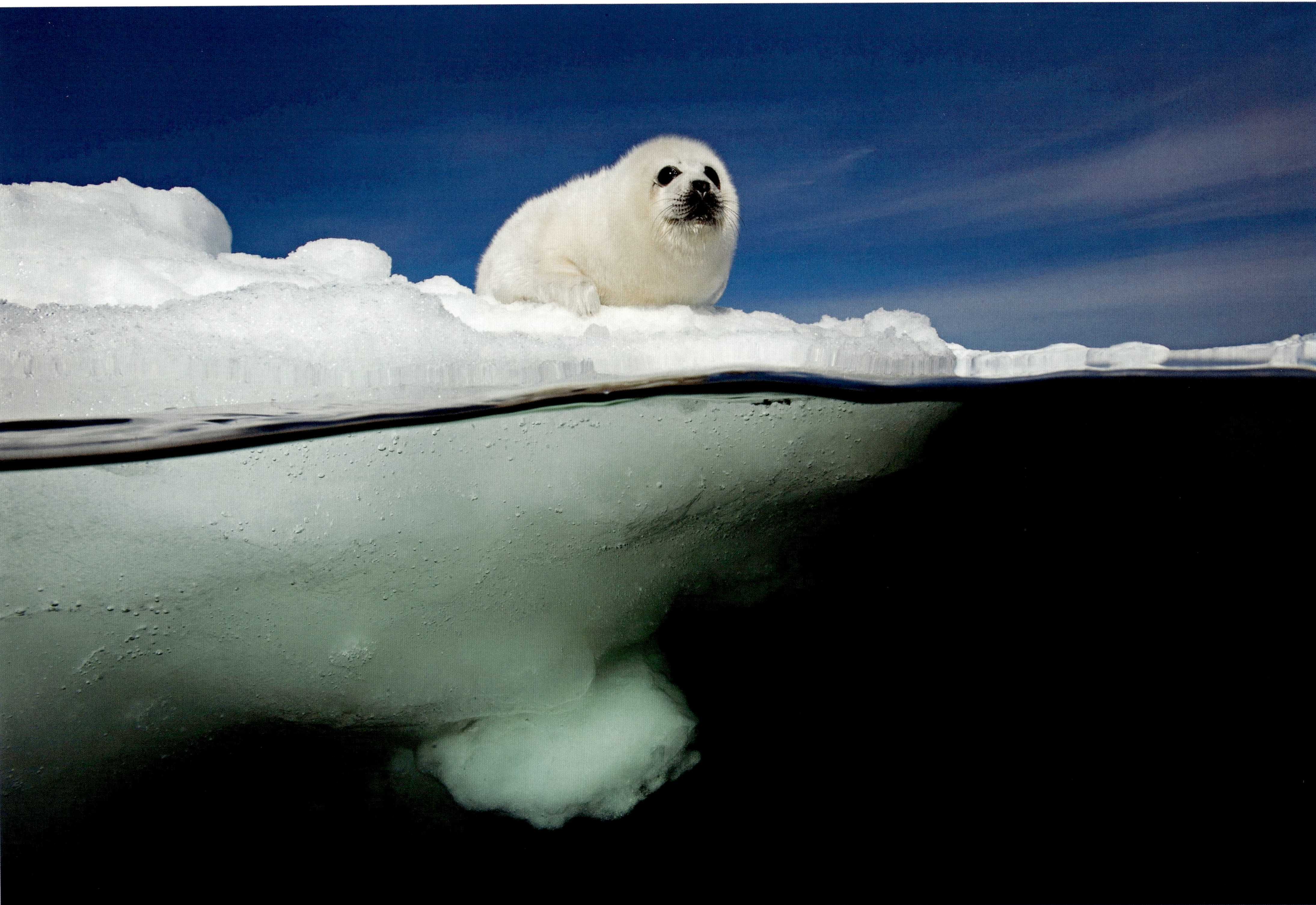

Harp Seal Pup, Gulf of St Lawrence, Canada, 2012

A harp seal pup peers into the icy sea, looking for its mother. The females nurse their pups a few times a day and then vanish beneath the sea ice, where they socialize and vocalize with other seals creating enchanting nonstop sound beneath the nursery. The mother's rich milk allows the pup to gain around 2 kilograms (4–5 pounds) per day, building a welcome reservoir of fat that will sustain the pup when the mother leaves.

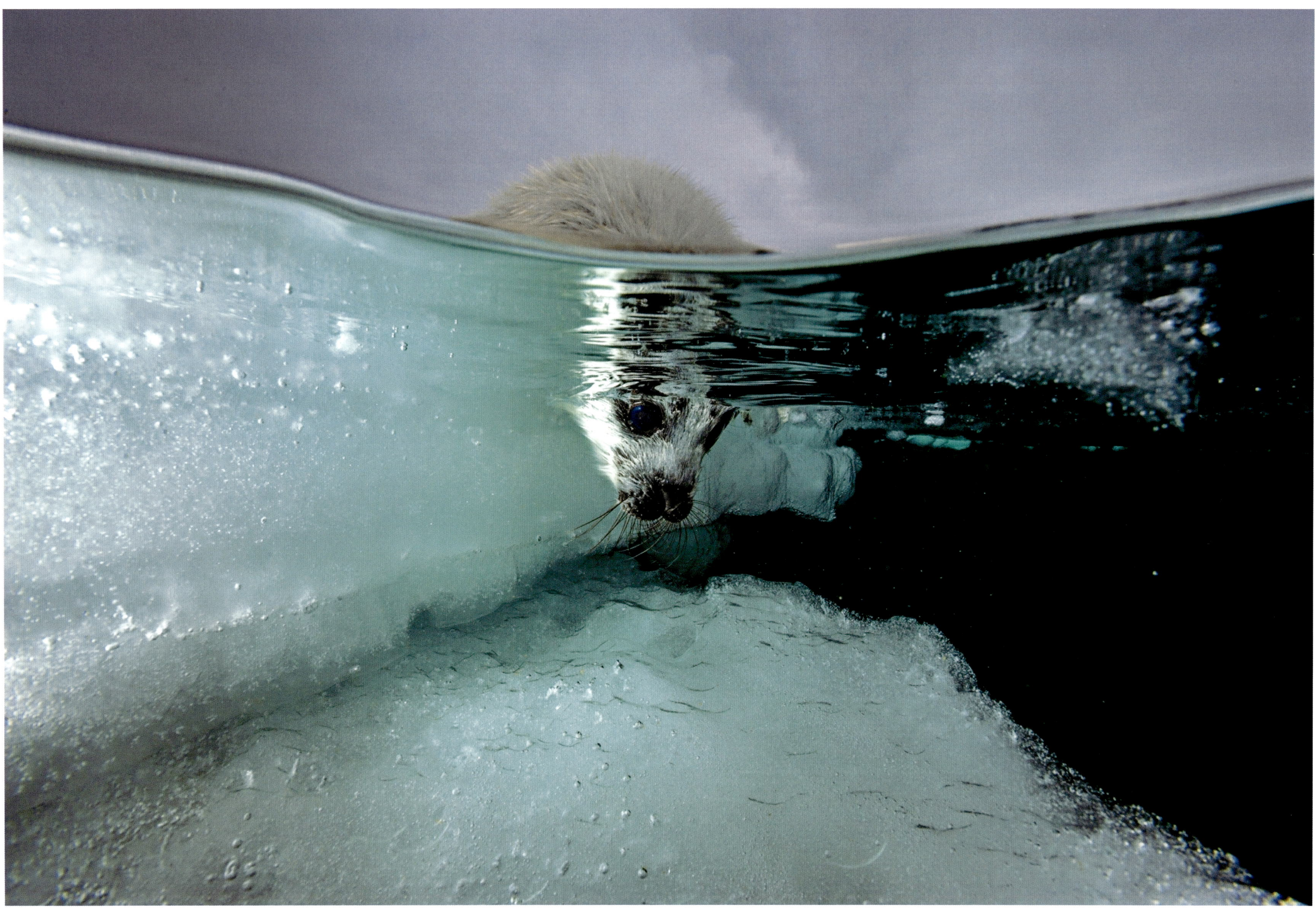

**Harp Seal Pup beneath Brooding Skies, Gulf of St Lawrence,
Canada, 2012**

An abandoned harp seal pup waits beneath storm-darkened skies for
a mother that has recently left and will not return to the ice to nurse.
The pup must rely on stored fat reserves and stable ice to survive until
it can fend for itself. Recent years of higher than normal temperatures
in the Gulf have disintegrated the nursery ice before the pups are mature
enough to survive.

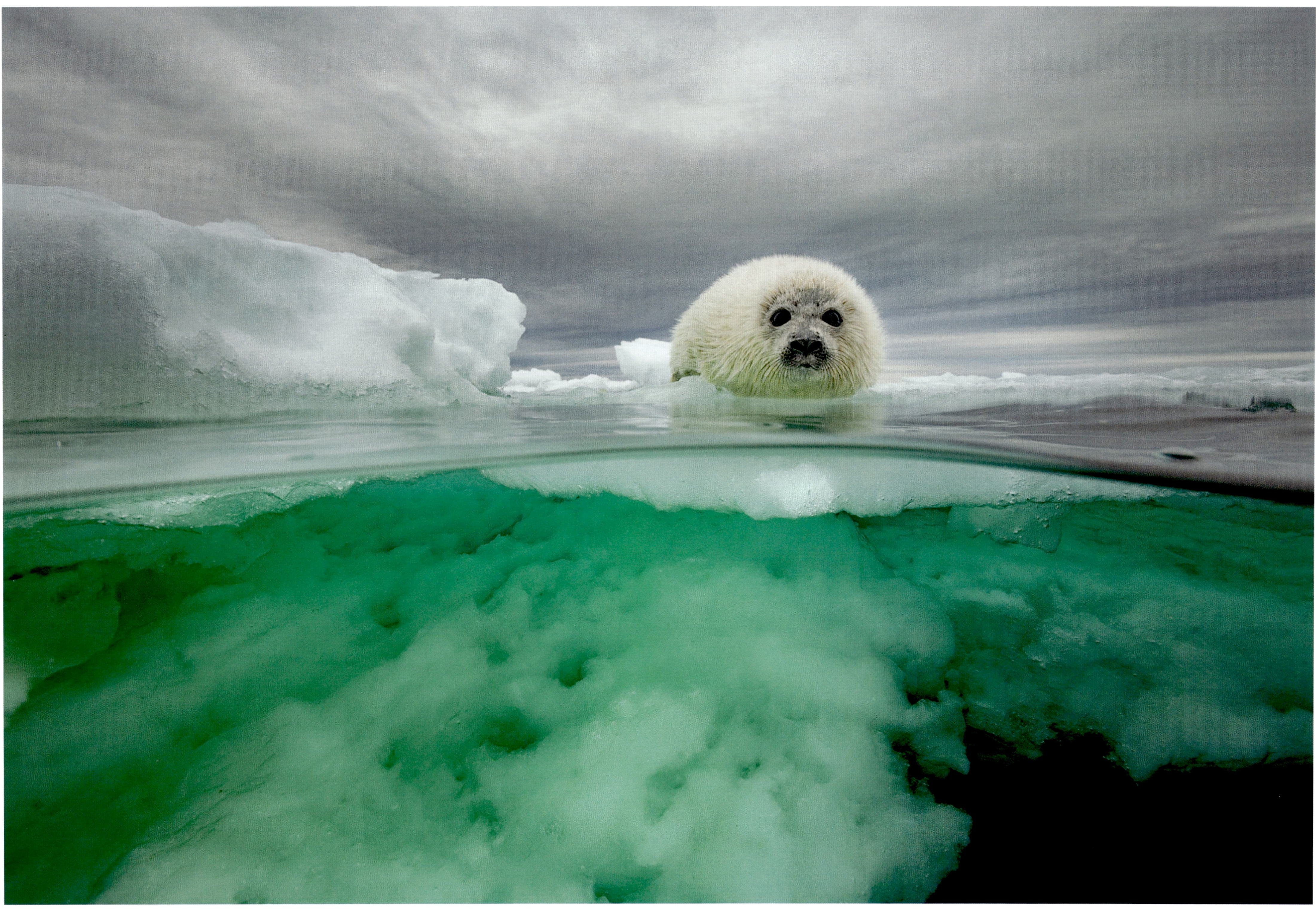

Harp Seal Pup, Gulf of St Lawrence, Canada, 2012

A harp seal pup explores its new ocean world as it learns to swim and
dive. As the days pass, the seals become sleek and agile swimmers if ice
conditions allow for their survival. We return to the Magdalen Islands in the
Gulf of St Lawrence every year that we can to continue to document the
harp seals. They are a face of climate change and may soon confront a Gulf
of St Lawrence without ice. Each time I descend into their shrinking world,
I am reminded that our daily choices have consequences.

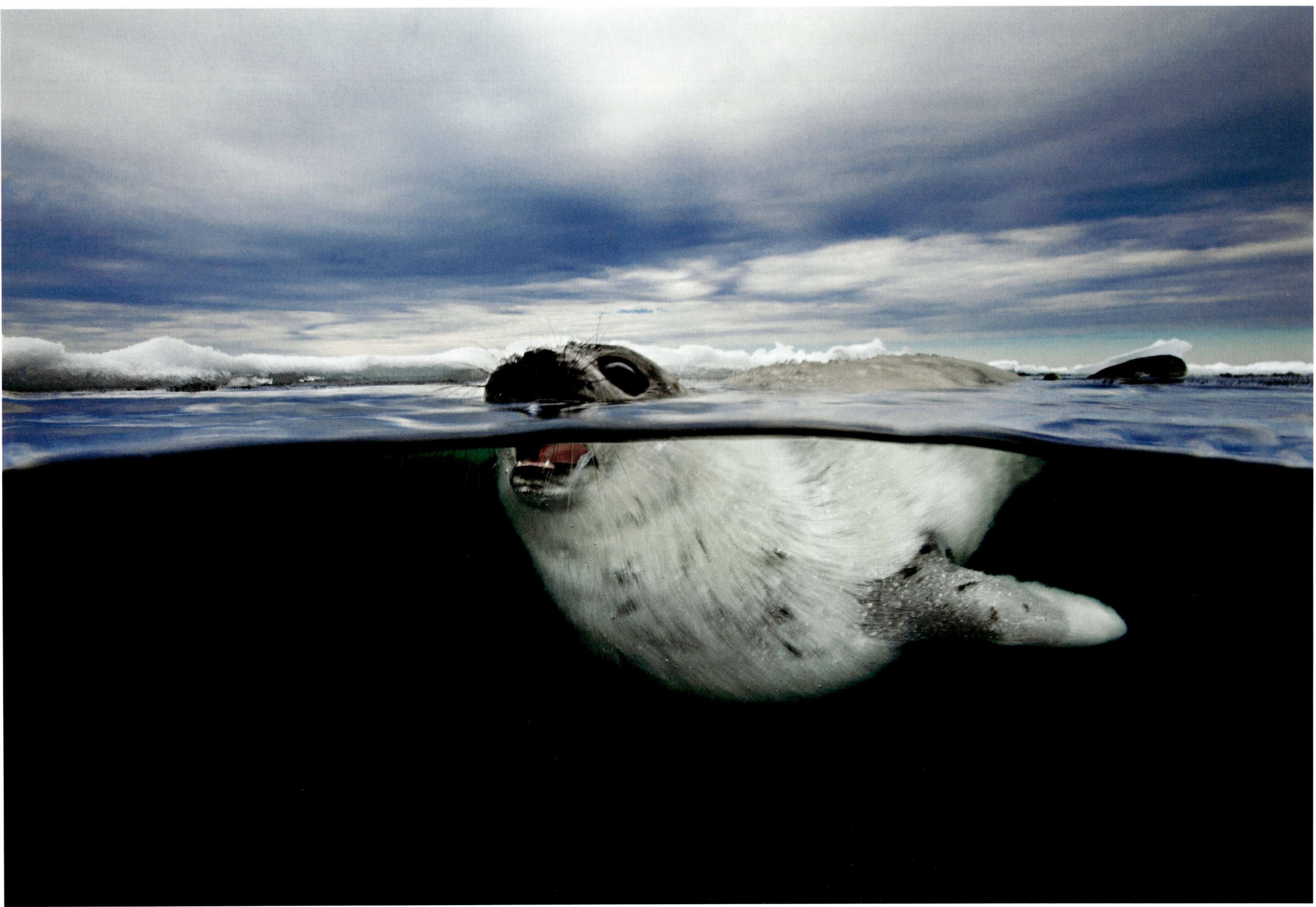

Opal Reef, Great Barrier Reef, Australia, 2009

A breaking wave reveals a secret coral garden on Opal Reef, near Port
Douglas, Queensland. The Great Barrier Reef is the world's most iconic
reef, a UNESCO World Heritage Site and the only biological structure
visible from space. The reef is also a victim of rising sea temperatures
related to climate change, resulting in coral bleaching events and
the death of corals in 2016, 2017 and 2020. I began photographing
this reef four decades ago, not realizing then that the pictures would
be a testament to coral through the lens of time.

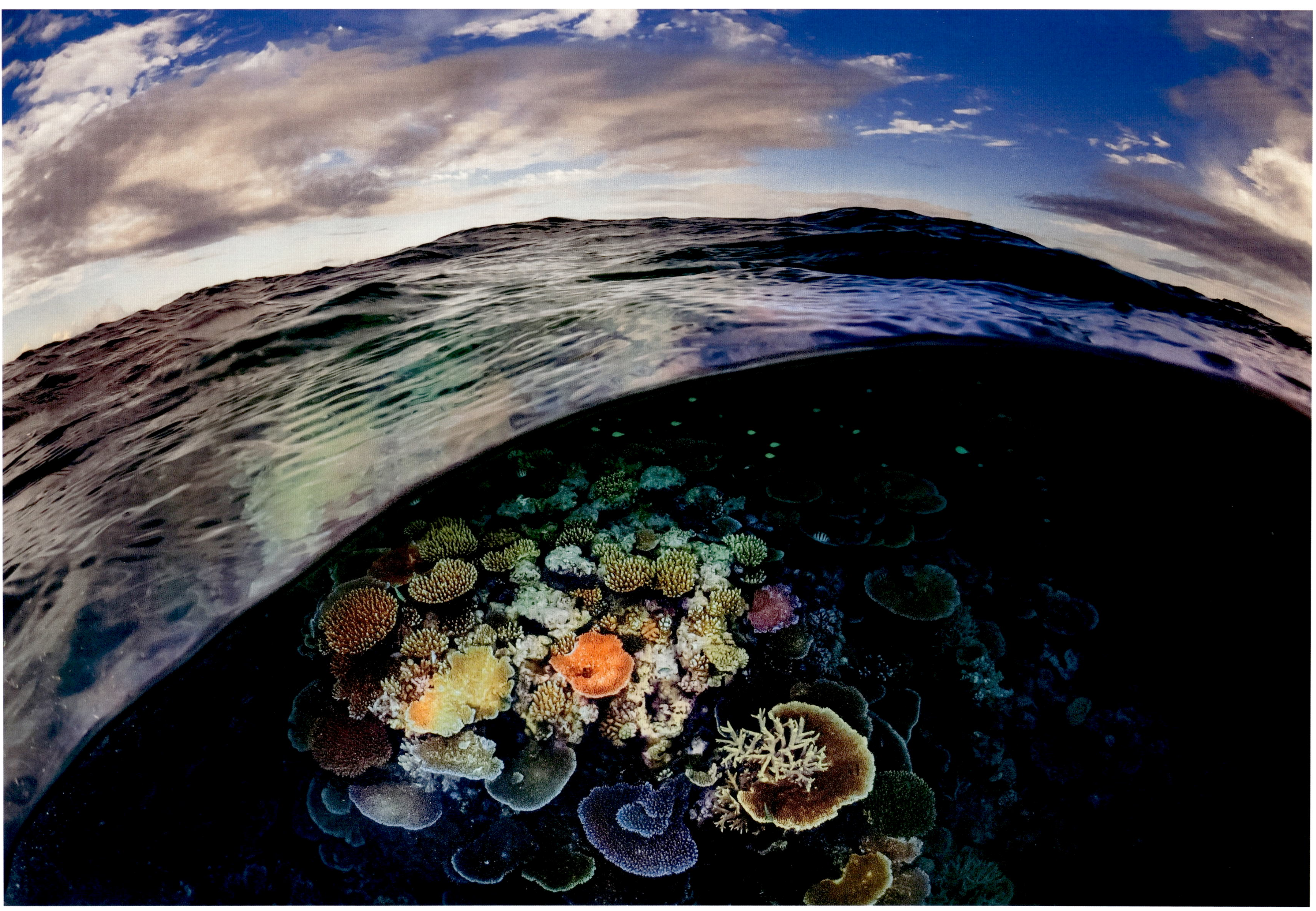

Double-Header Wrasse, Lord Howe Island, Australia, 1990

A double-header wrasse (*Coris bulbifrons*) patrols a coral-fringed
lagoon on Lord Howe Island, a remote volcanic remnant in the Tasman
Sea, located southeast of Australia's coast. This UNESCO World
Heritage Site is a temperate island bathed in warm currents that support
the southernmost coral reefs on the planet.

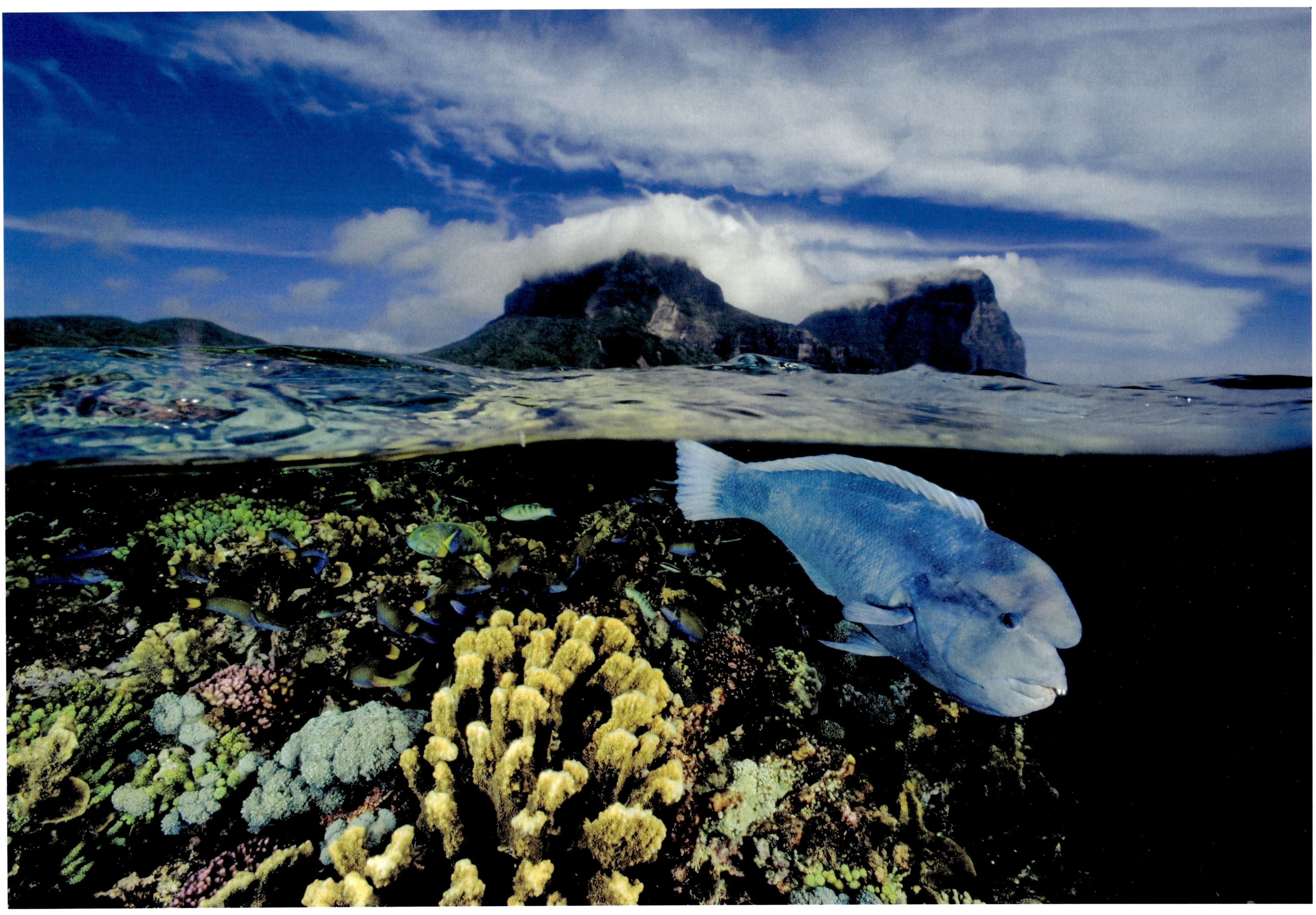

Sand Cay and Coral, Great Barrier Reef, Australia, 1999

This fiercely white sand cay appears almost like an iceberg or a distant
mountain, crowning a pastel pasture of corals on the northern reaches of
the Great Barrier Reef. At low tide, the cay is a resting place for sea birds
but it nearly vanishes at high tide. These small cays are elevated islets of
sand sitting above the reef that can shift, shrink or grow in size at the will
of storms, waves and currents.

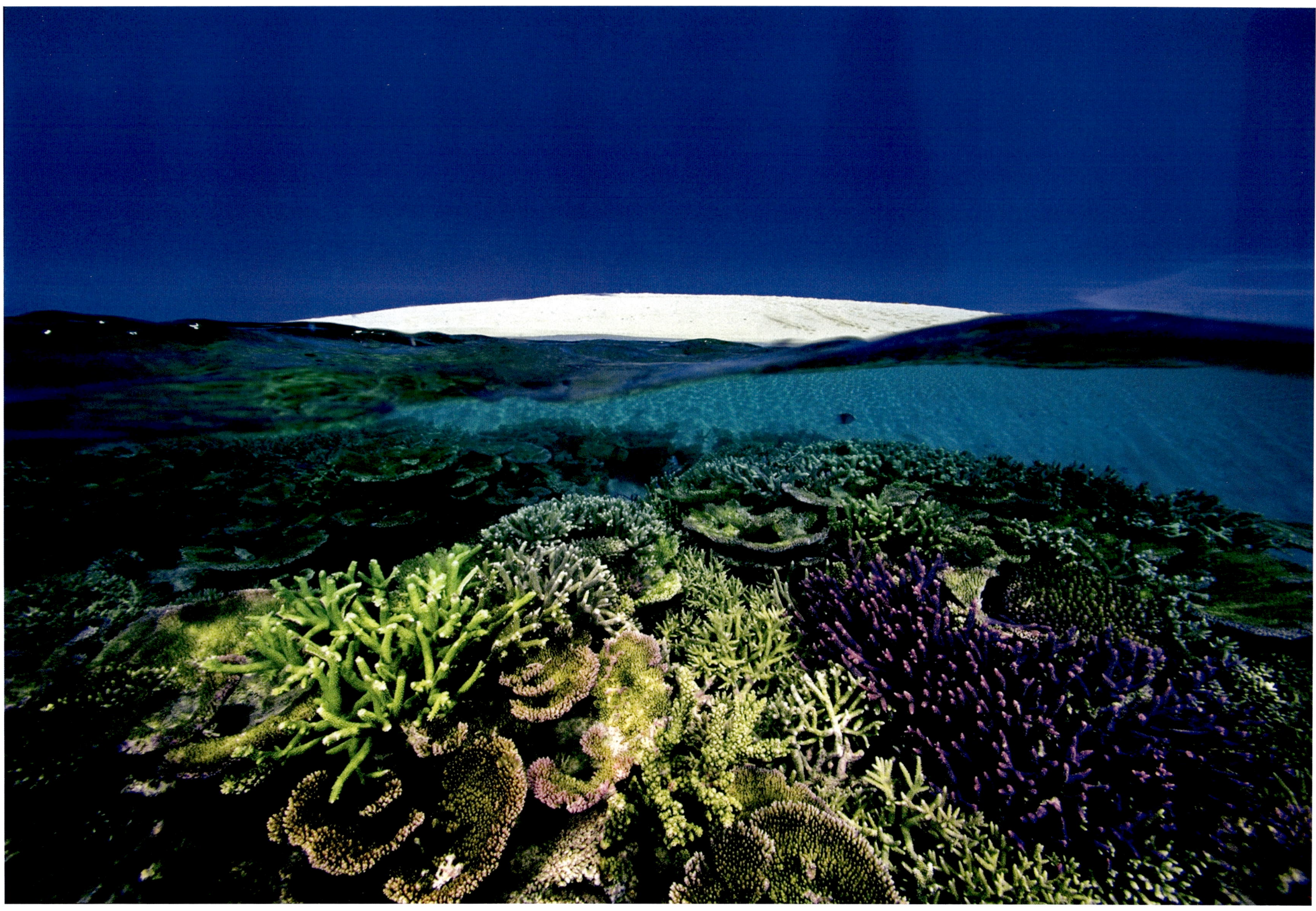

Elephantfish Fishery, Tasmania, Australia, 1995

A fisherman uses a gillnet to catch elephantfish (*Callorhinchus milii*, also known as elephant or ghost shark) in the shallows of Hobart Sound. Like many creatures in these temperate waters, elephantfish seem like the stuff of our imagination: they have no scales, are silky to the touch and sport a pachyderm-like proboscis filled with sensory receptors. In the spring they rise from the deep to lay pairs of leathery eggs in the shallows.

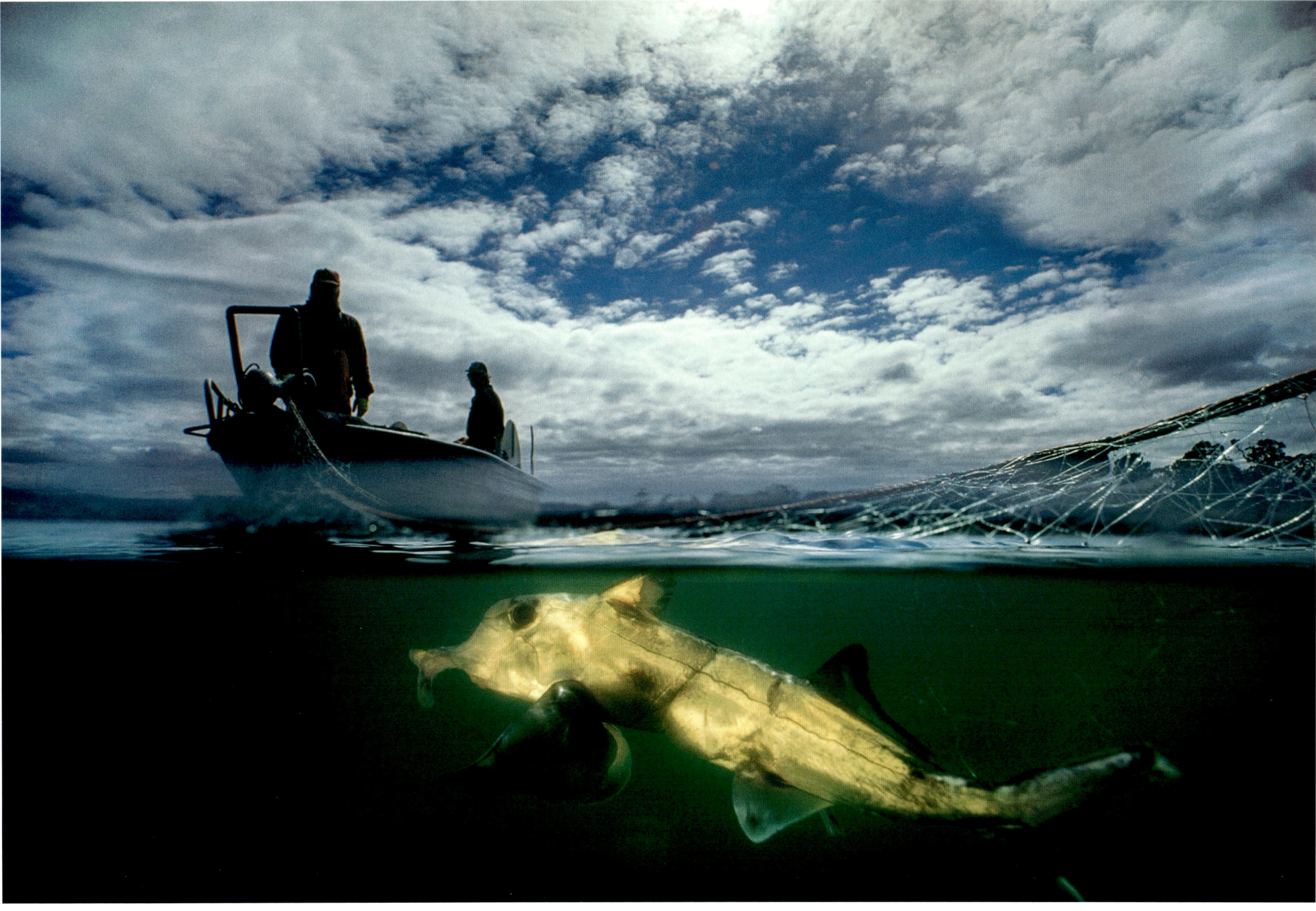

Ocean Plastics, Anilao, Philippines, 2017

Our addiction to plastic has created an unprecedented environmental problem: our plastic footprint will outlive us on this planet.

We were diving near a small fishing community in Anilao, on the southern end of the Calumpang Peninsula, when the tide delivered a floating cloud of plastic into the small cove. Around the world, eight million tons of plastic enter our oceans every year. It is a global problem that requires a global solution, but an important part of that is an individual's choice to reduce, recycle and reuse.

Coral Reef, Tumon Bay Marine Preserve, Guam, 2005 and 2017
(overleaf, left and right)

Framed against a blue sky, hotel buildings rise behind a complex labyrinth of healthy coral reefs in Tumon Bay. This marine preserve is bathed in astoundingly clear waters from the nearby Mariana Trench, the deepest reaches of our planet. Unlike many other offshore reefs, visitors can explore these corals and the creatures that live here by taking a short wade and then a swim from the beach. Working here, you can watch octopuses and reef fish patrolling below while listening to conversations from the hotels wafting across the waves.

Coral reefs are a thermometer of our oceans. I returned to Tumon Bay with a *National Geographic* grant to explore coral through the lens of time. I wanted to revisit reefs I had previously documented and continue to tell their story through photography and time. Unprecedented thermal spikes between 2013 and 2017 had caused the Tumon Bay reefs to lose their symbiotic algae in a process called coral bleaching. I swam out to the same spot I shot in 2005, but the familiar skyline was now rising above heat-ravaged reefs. Combined with extreme low tides, shallow reefs could not recover from a succession of heat stress. Once reaching for the sun, the corals had bleached, died and begun to collapse on themselves like grey concrete. Even more startling than the coral's appearance was the silence beneath the surface, evidence of not only the destruction of the coral itself but also its once-thriving ecosystem.

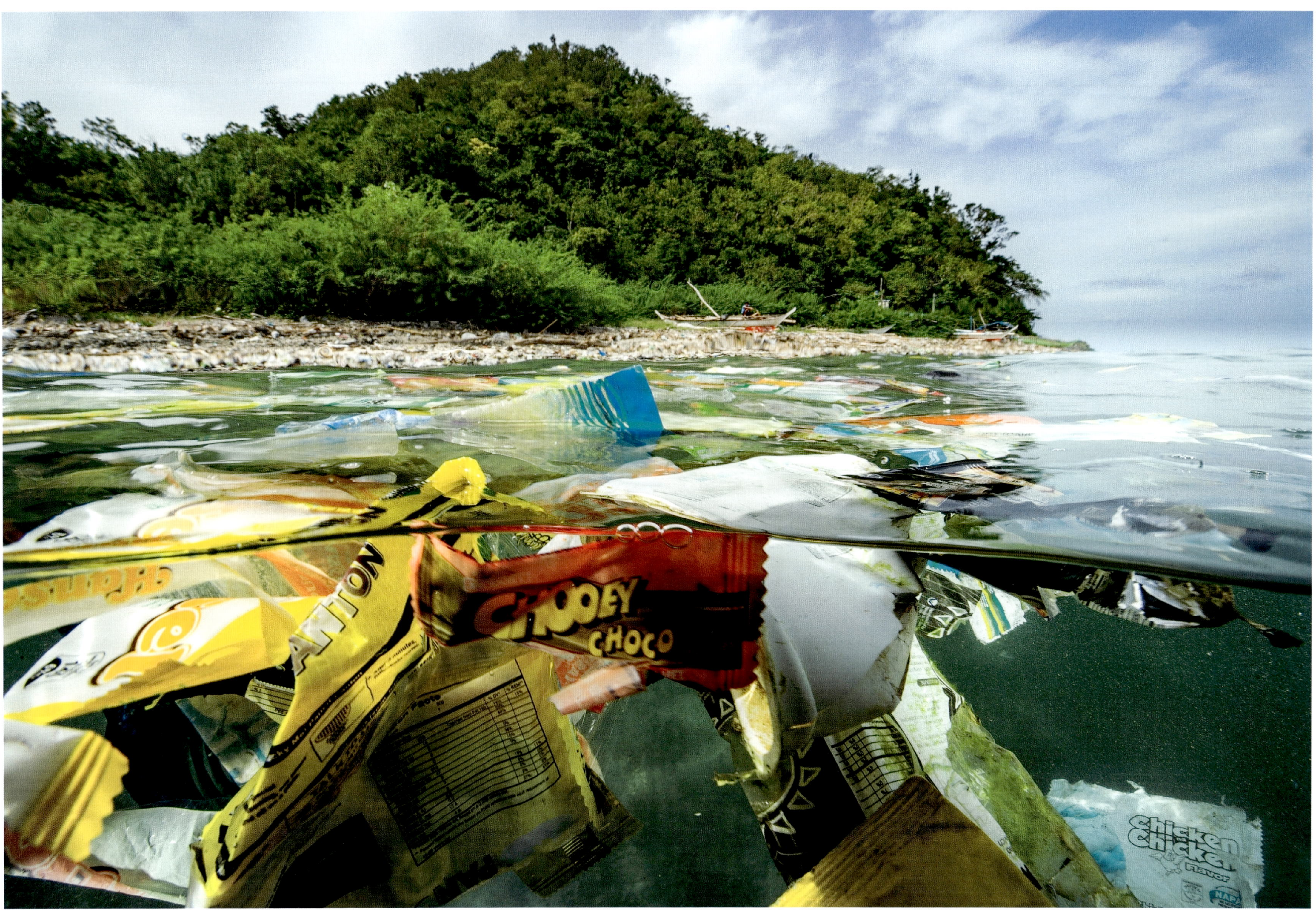

CHOOEY
CHOCO
Chicken
Chicken
Flavor

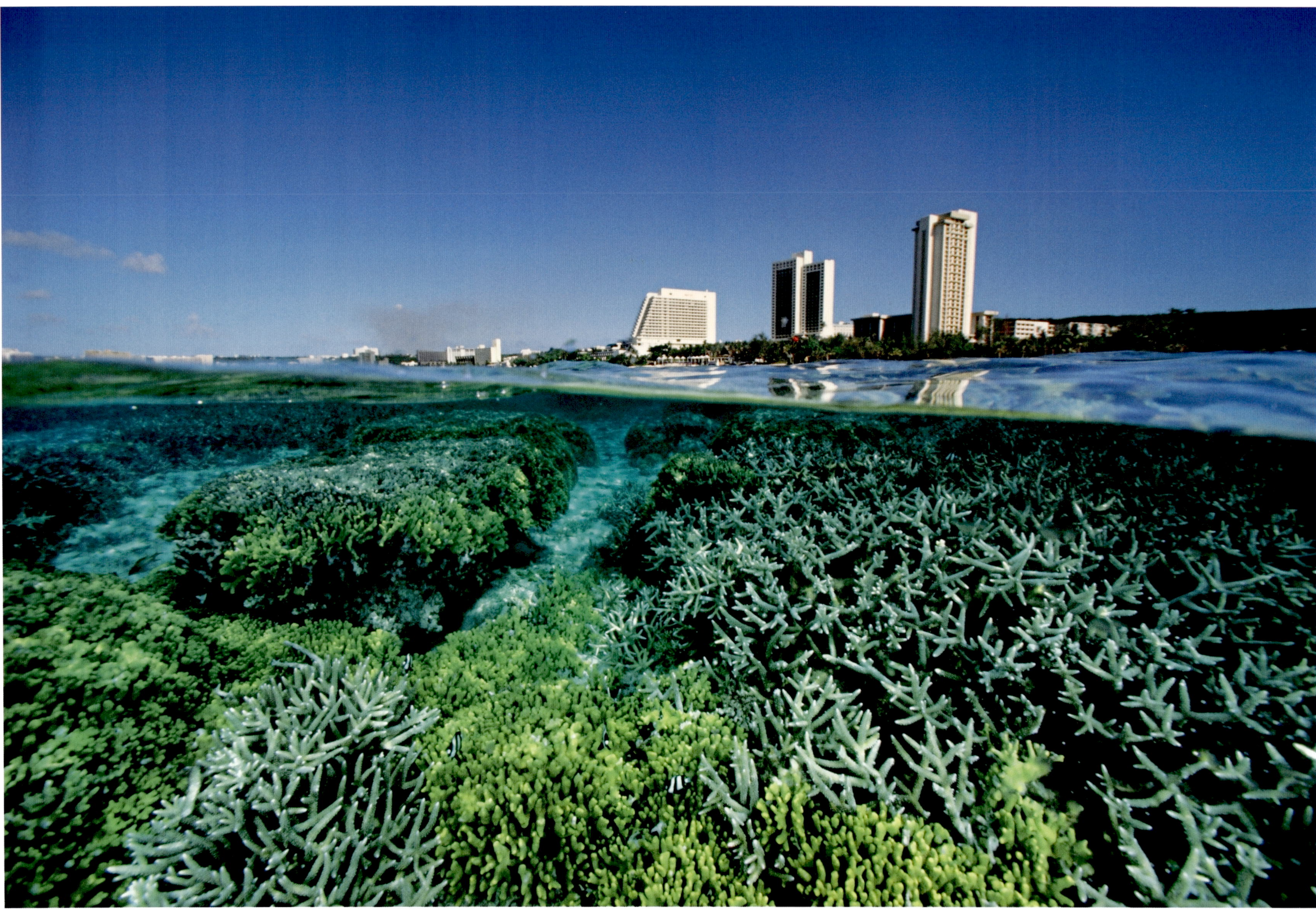

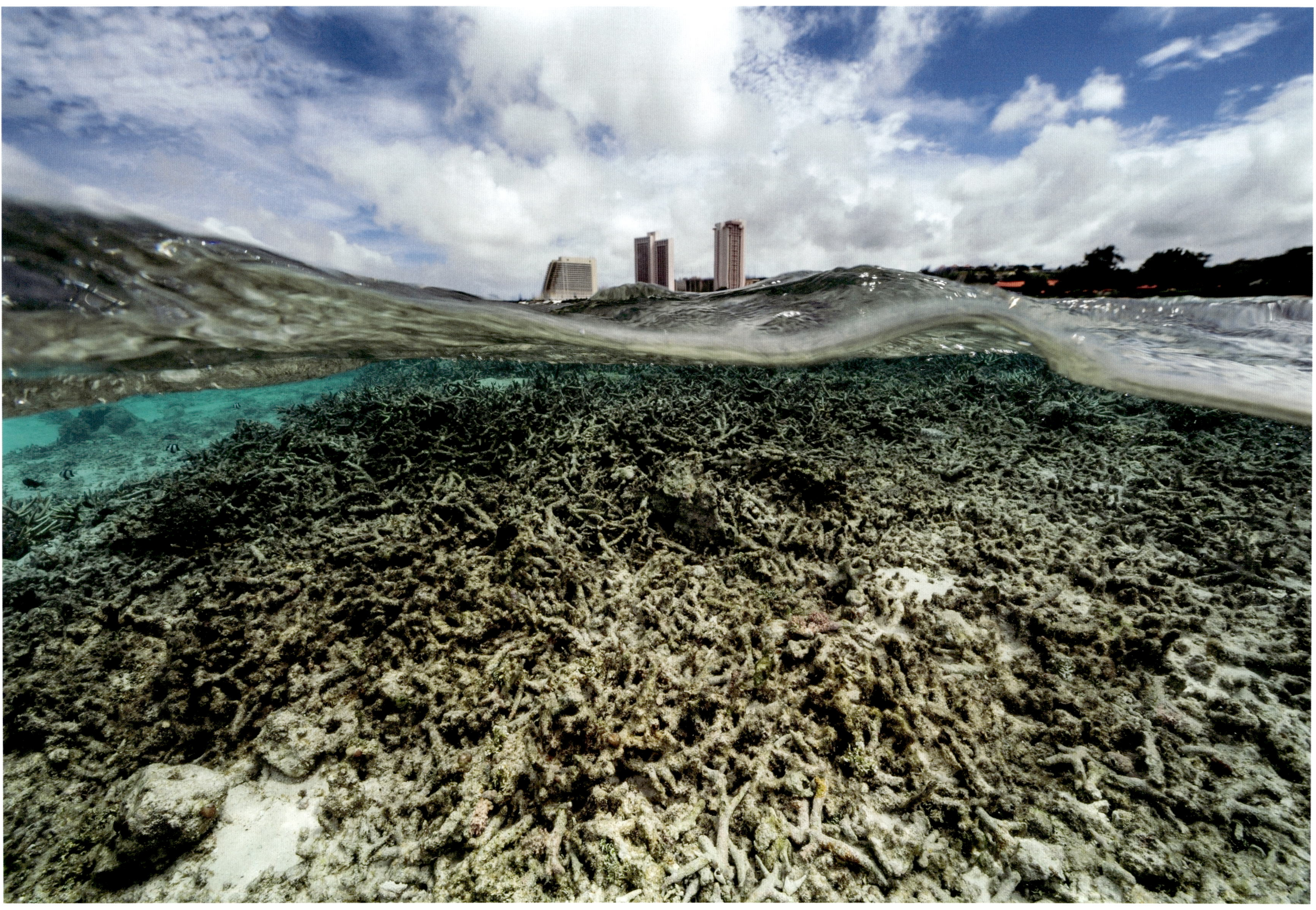

A lion's mane jellyfish (*Cyanea capillata*) hunts in the shadow of the first commercial offshore wind farm in the United States, located off Block Island, Rhode Island. We descended beneath the turbines and found schools of fish clustering at the base. In addition to contributing clean, renewable energy, the wind farm is creating habitat as an unexpected artificial reef.

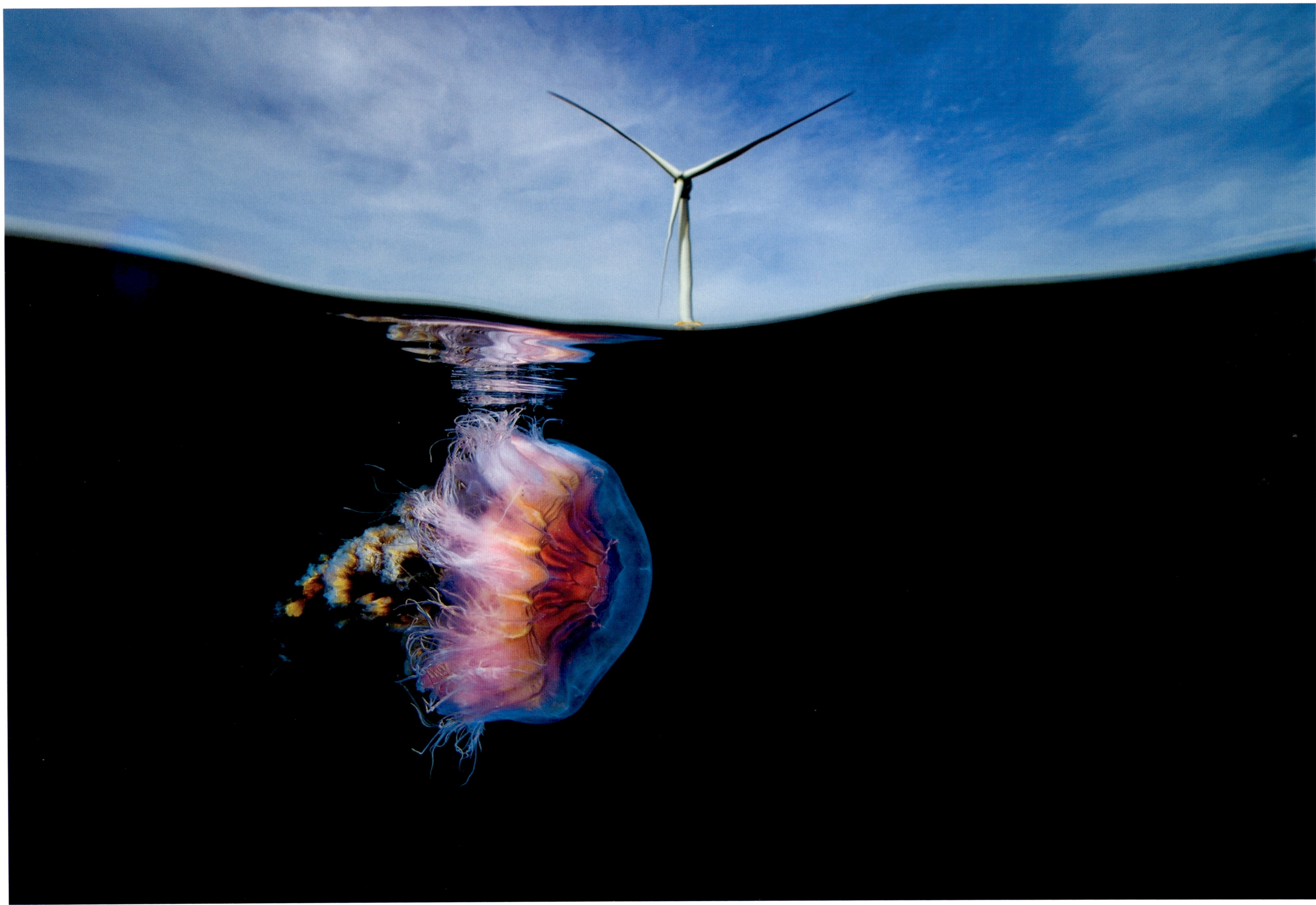

**Brown Boobies, Tubbataha Reefs Natural Park, Palawan,
Philippines, 2016**

Brown boobies (*Sula leucogaster*) seek a moment of rest on a coral
pyramid that will soon vanish with the rising tide in Tubbataha Reefs
Natural Park, one of the last seabird rookeries in the Philippines. As
creatures of sea and sky, these birds play an integral part of the reef
system as important as fish and coral. Photographing them from sea
level requires infinite stealth, silence, patience and, ultimately, luck.

Whale Shark, Oslob, Philippines, 2016
(overleaf, left and right)

A whale shark (*Rhincodon typus*) rises toward an outrigger, hopeful for
a handful of krill near Oslob, Philippines. Hundreds of people arrive each
day to snorkel with these gentle giants. Operations purposefully cease
by late morning, encouraging the whale sharks to swim off to the depths.
The practice of feeding whale sharks is controversial. Supporters feel
the sharks are ocean ambassadors, while scientists debate the impact of
feeding on their behaviour.

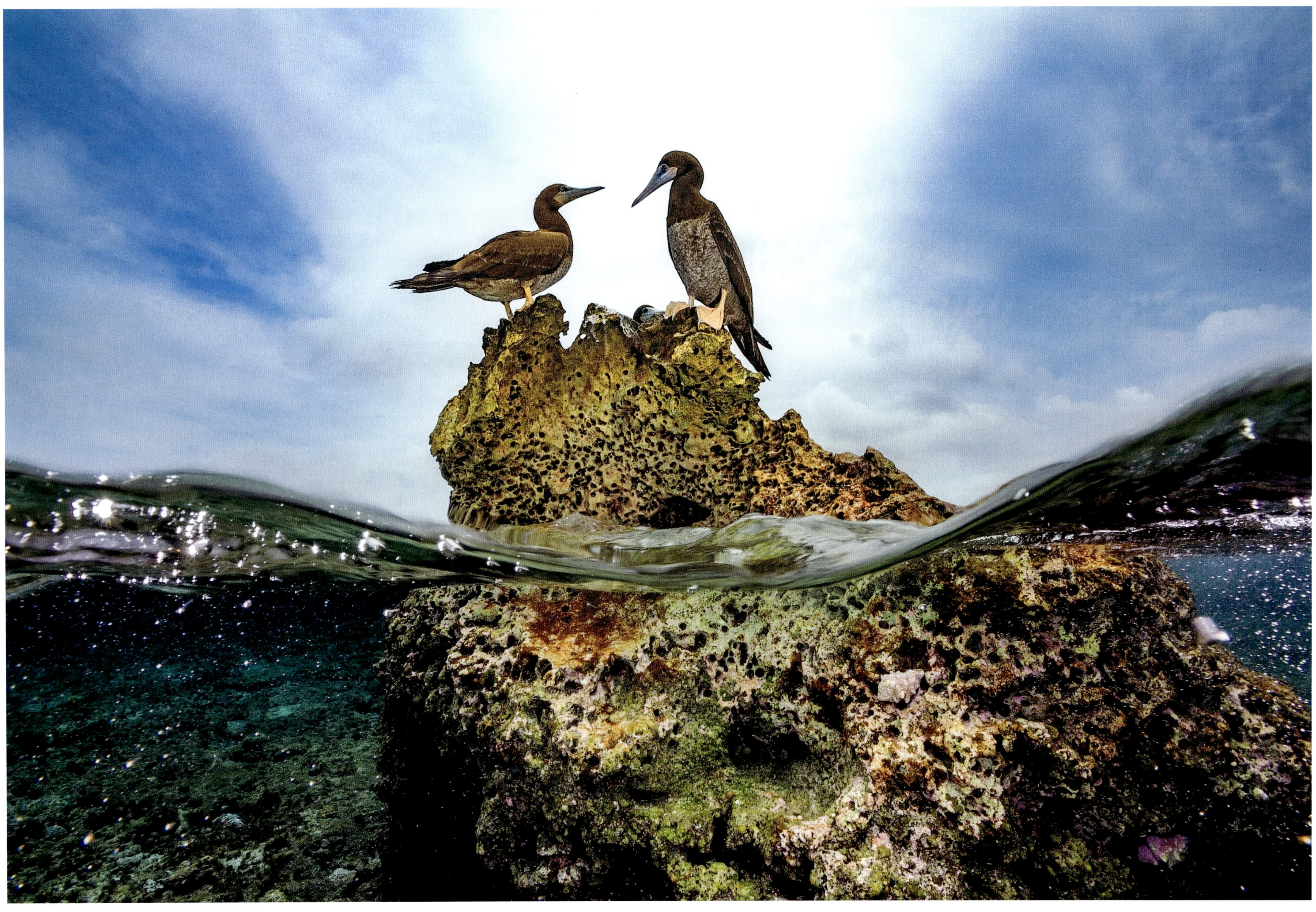

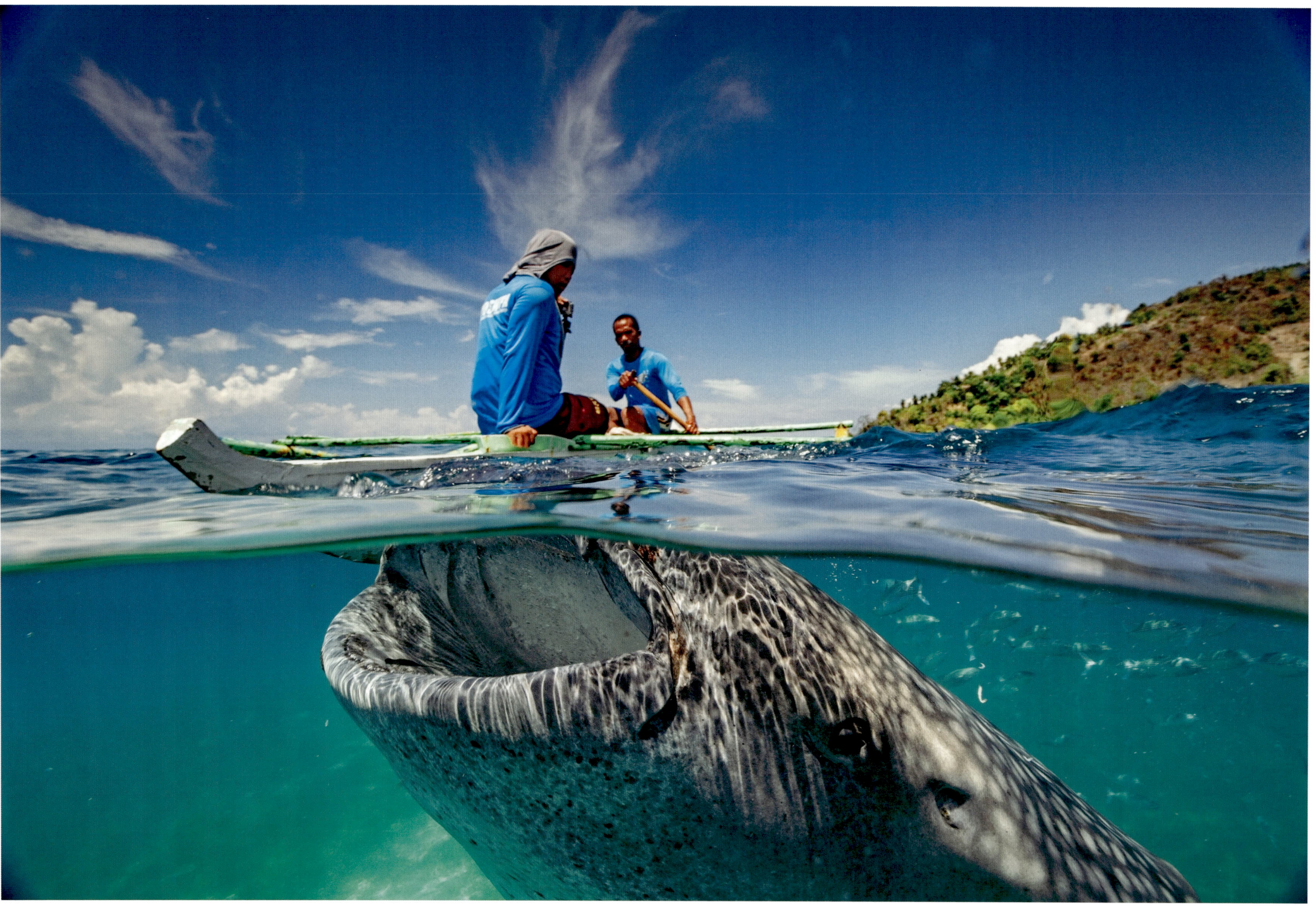

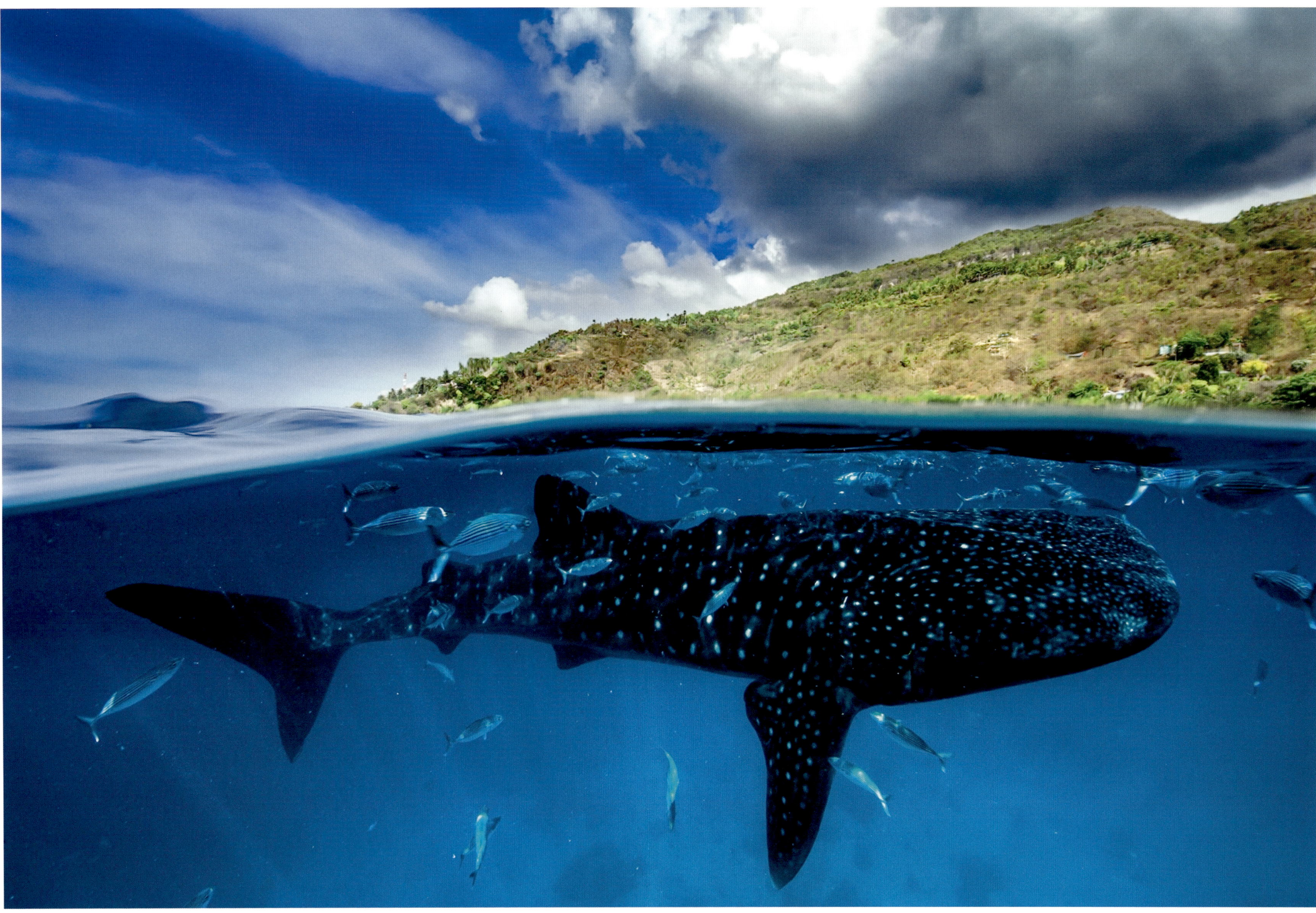

Forests of delicate staghorn corals (*Acropora cervicornis*) reach toward a technicolour sky in the lagoon surrounding the Ranger Station, an outpost perched on the southernmost tip of North Atoll. This isolated and storm-tossed area is accessible to liveaboard diving expeditions for only three months of the year. However, it is protected year-round by a team of dedicated rangers who guard these wild waters against poachers, under the direction of Superintendent Angelique Songco.

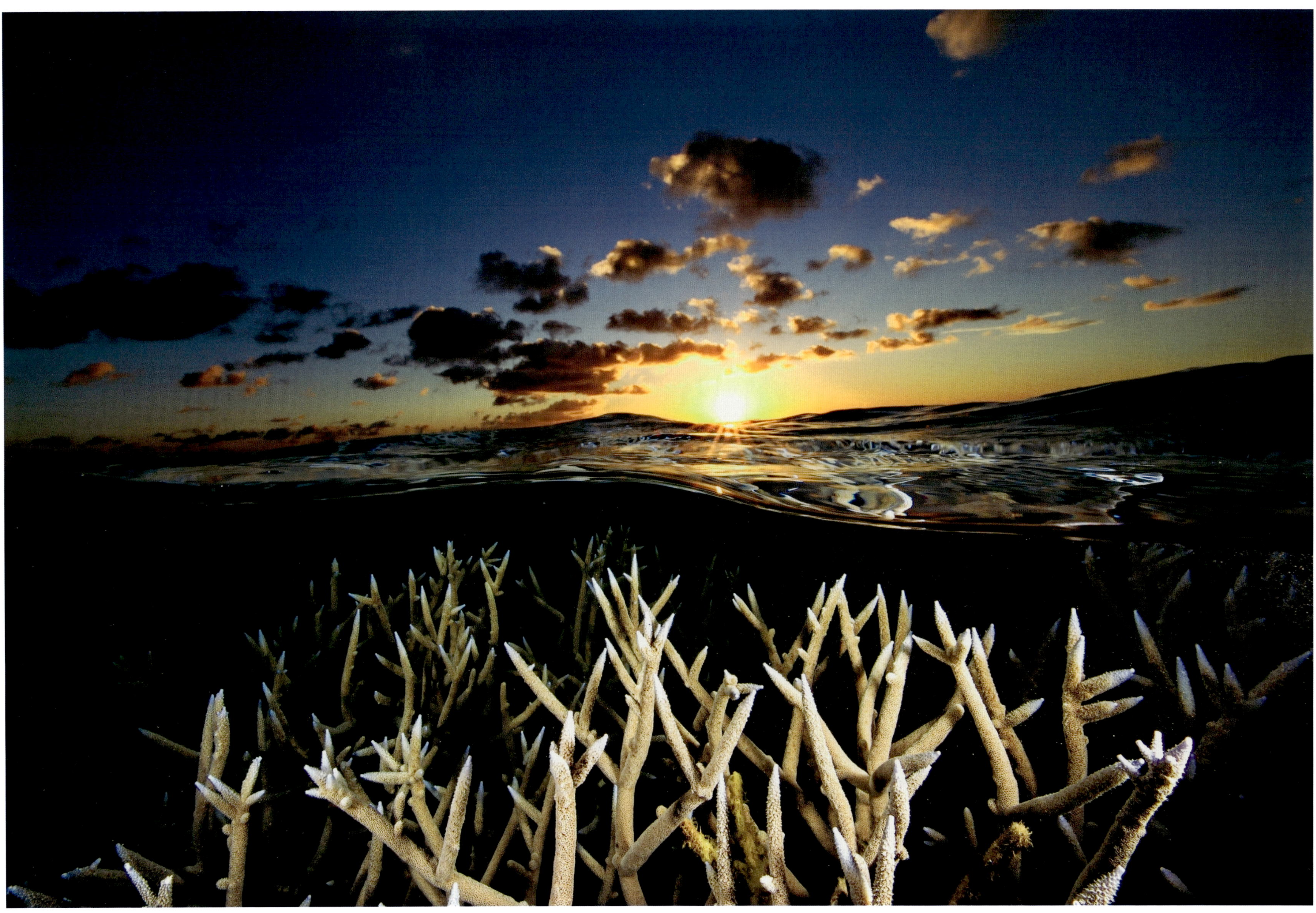

Our team was heading back to Kri Island after a torrential rain when we encountered a few fishermen in their small wooden outriggers gathered near a tiny, mushroom-shaped islet. We were drenched and tired, but something inside me said, 'Stop the boat and get in the water'. The sea appeared empty but I hovered just below the surface and could not believe my eyes. Millions of baitfish had formed a silver carousel that circled around and around the island. The fisherman stood, creating a dark statue silhouetted against a clearing evening sky.

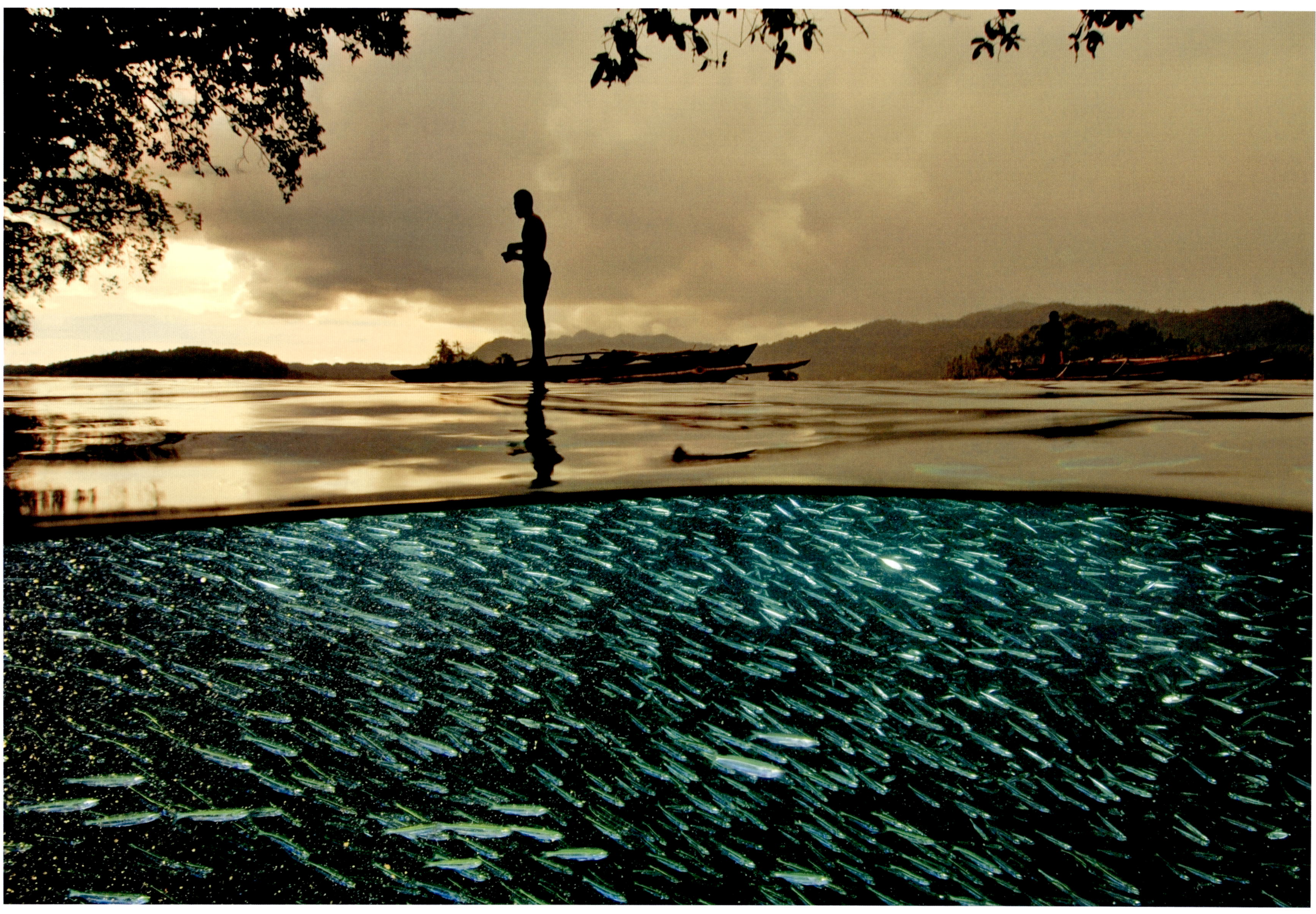

Moon Jellyfish, Gam Island, Raja Ampat, Republic of Indonesia, 2006

Max Ammer – founder of Papua Diving and a pioneering diver in the
waters of Raja Ampat – mentioned that he had something special to share
with us. We loaded our gear into his boat and headed for Gam Island. He
slowed to a drift as we entered a cove pulsing with thousands of jellyfish.
I slid in at twilight and turned to see a fisherman passing over this alien
world of ghostly white moon jellyfish (*Aurelia aurita*).

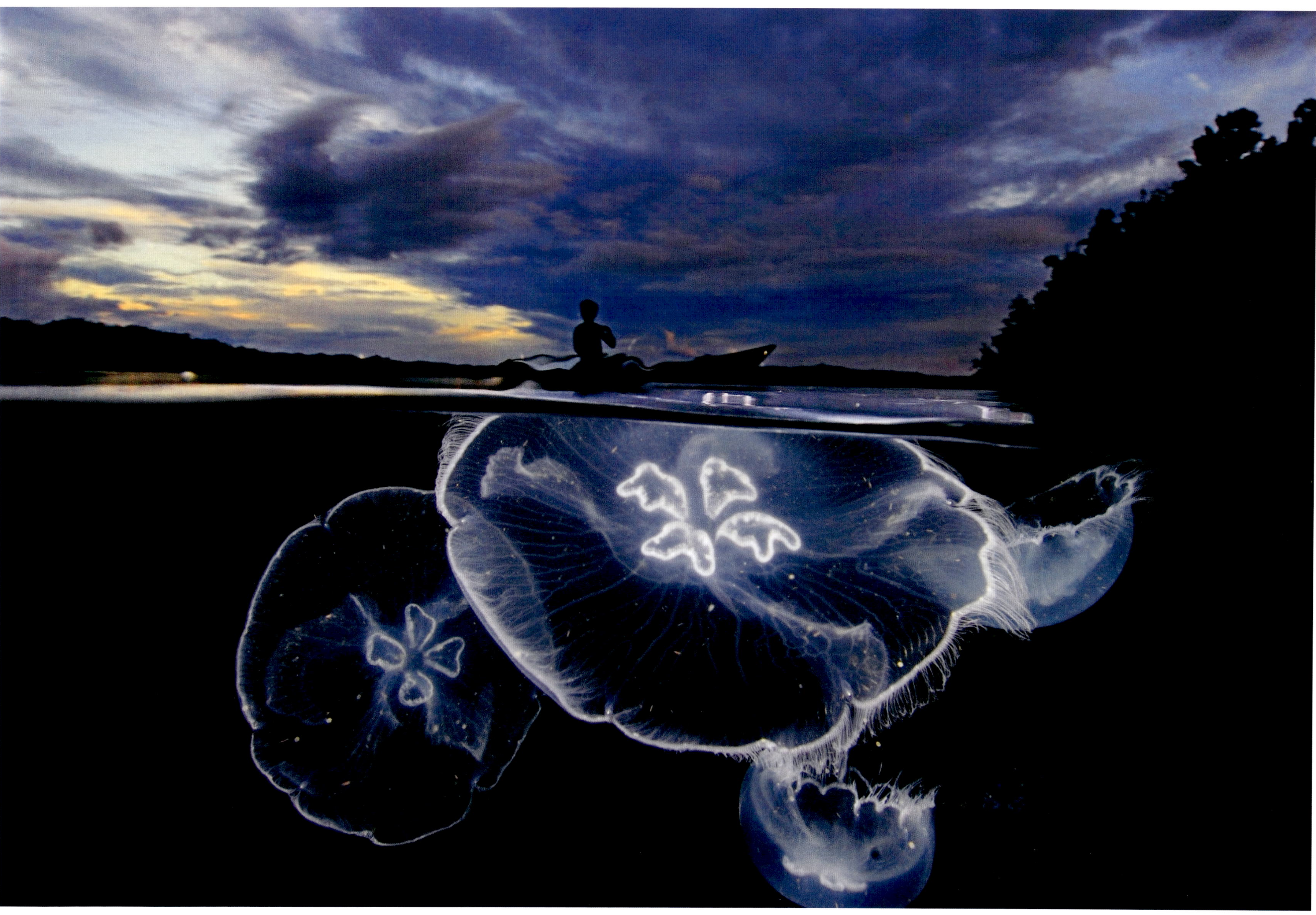

Reef and Rainforest, Raja Ampat, Republic of Indonesia, 2018

I swam into a small cove and was transfixed by the coral in aquarium-clear water and the rainforest-covered tower rising above a secluded beach. As I photographed, I wondered how many people, if any, had stepped onto this private paradise that disappears beneath a high tide. When we first came to Raja Ampat in 2005, we did not see another boat during a month at sea. Now, the exponential growth of ocean-related ecotourism supports community conservation efforts that sustain multiple protected areas.

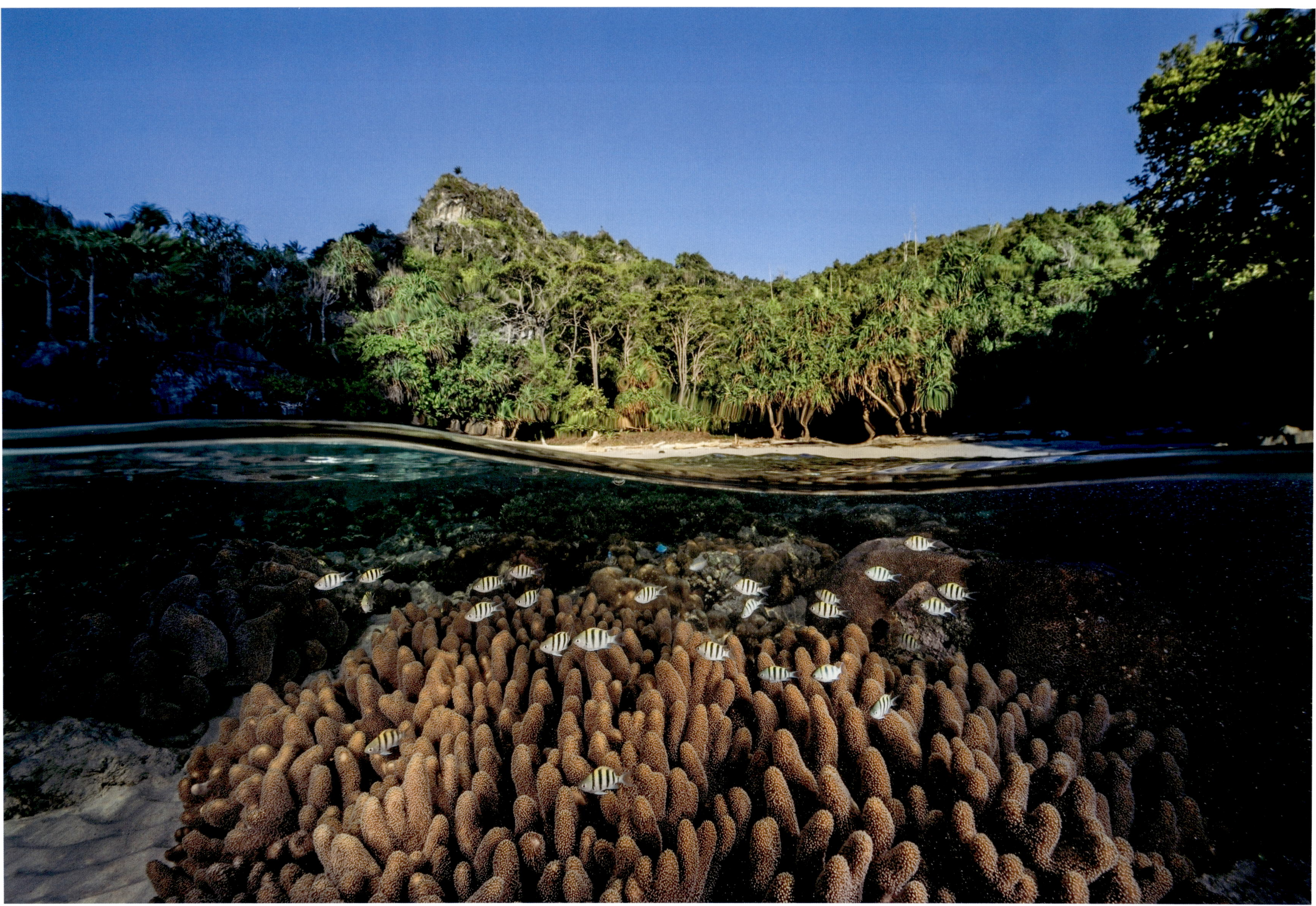

Mangrove, Kri Island, Raja Ampat, Republic of Indonesia, 2006

A rainforest-covered mountain slopes down to a calm, clear mangrove carpeted with a dense but delicate spread of leather corals. Staring through the viewfinder, I was completely fascinated by the incredible shades of green in this secret garden that linked the sea to the surface.

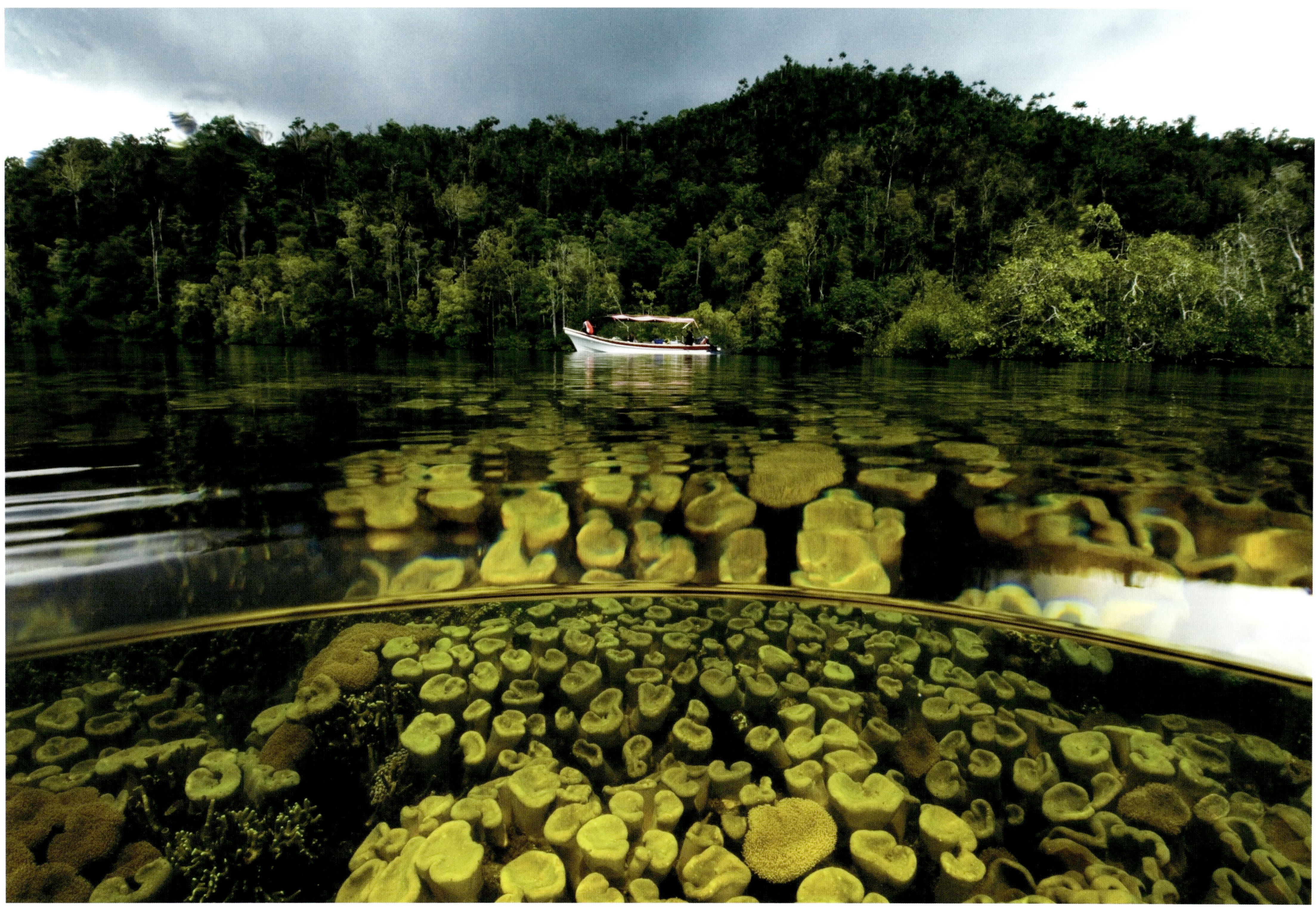

Coral and Clouds, Republic of Palau, 2019

A threatening storm brought wind and rising waves, revealing large coral
fields that stretched as far as the eye could see. Palau, a jewel in the
Pacific dedicated to protecting its ocean resources, was the first nation to
declare its waters a shark sanctuary. It is a place of marine lakes filled with
jellyfish, blue corner drop-offs, great mating aggregations and manta-filled
channels. Even though I have spent decades returning to these waters,
I find that every dive is still a voyage of discovery.

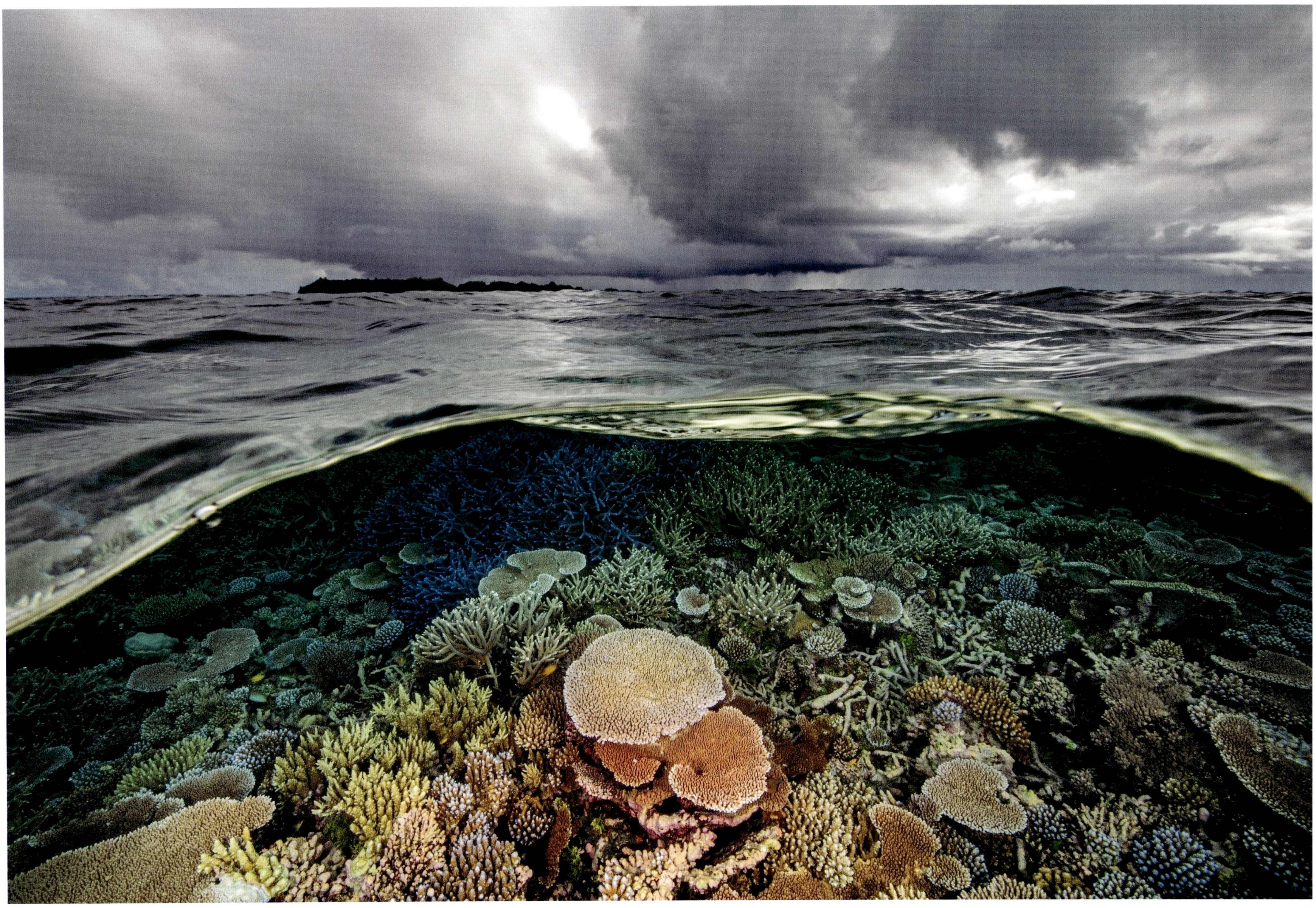

Next-Generation Ocean, Republic of Palau, 2019

Palau is a global leader in marine conservation. As of January 2020,
the Palau National Marine Sanctuary protects eighty per cent of its
national waters to support economic and environmental sustainability
for generations to come. This is a small island nation with perhaps the
world's biggest commitment to conservation. I witnessed these Palauan
children explore their marine heritage beneath a jungle-covered
limestone islet.

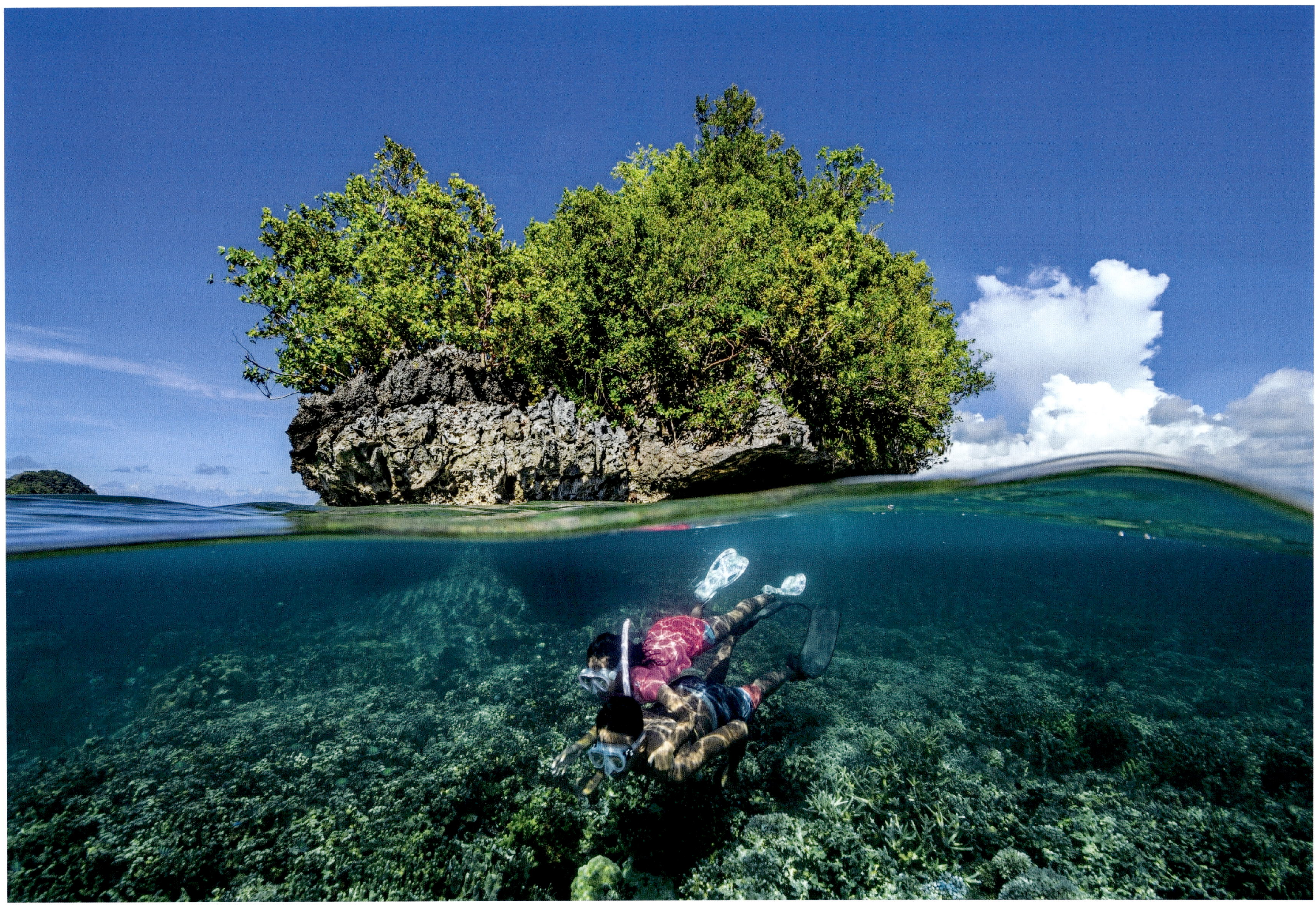

Satawal Island, located in Micronesia's Caroline Islands, is a tiny speck in
the great Pacific. Yet this small coral atoll was home to many extraordinary
master navigators who once sailed vast oceans in traditional canoes
without modern instrumentation, relying instead upon the sun, stars, wind,
waves, currents and marine life to guide them. A group of children on
the beach followed me into the water as I explored the island from the sea.
I turned to see the descendants of these ancient wayfinders at home in
their ocean.

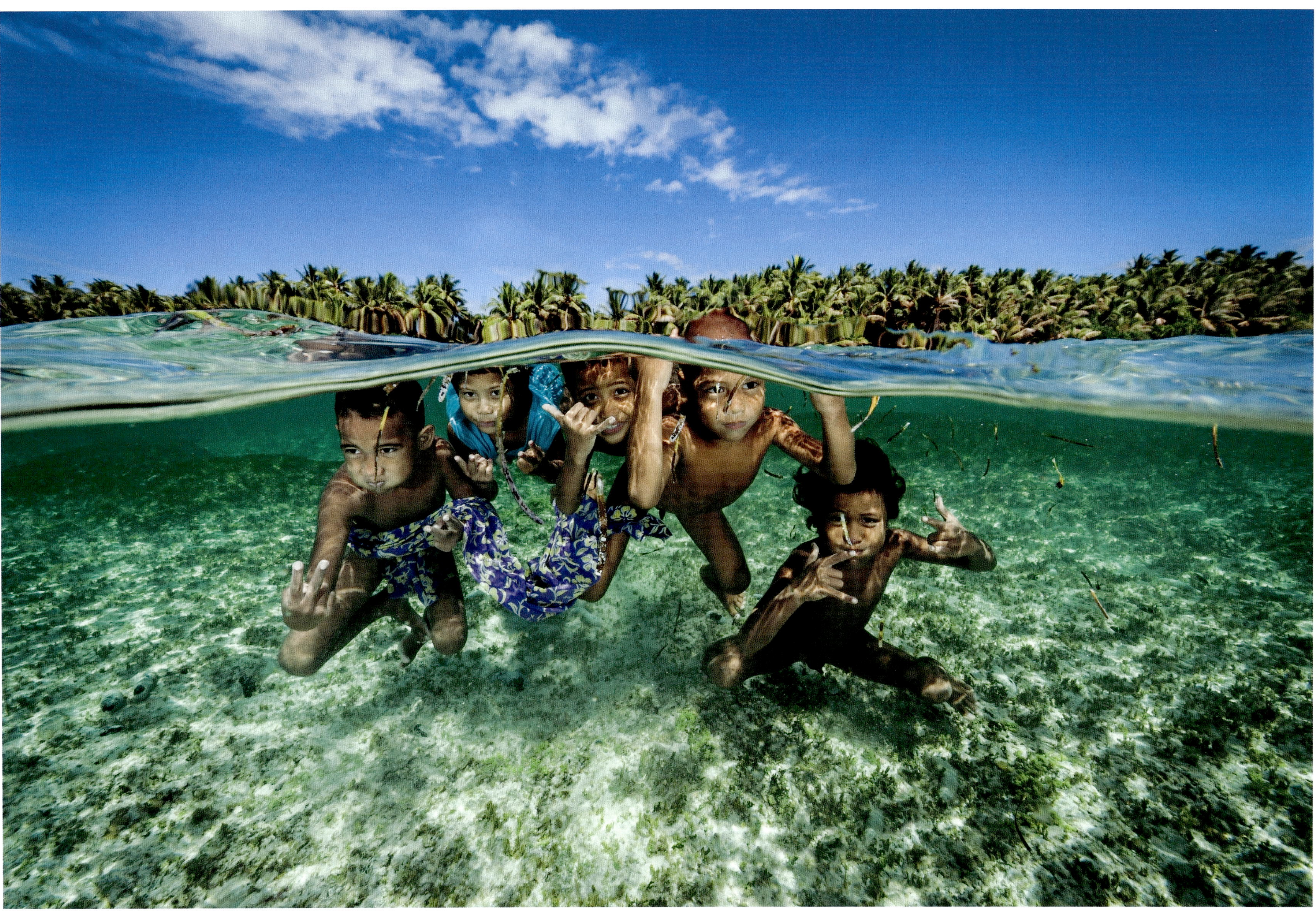

Father and Son, Kimbe Bay, Papua New Guinea, 2013

I returned to Kimbe Bay after my first expedition there seventeen years
earlier to discover the reefs had continued to flourish. This corner of
the Coral Triangle is a deep basin punctuated by unique coral-covered
seamounts and vibrant reef slopes. After a few attempts, I was still
searching for the right place to make a half-and-half image that captured
the essence of this place. Max Benjamin at Walindi Plantation suggested
a distant island near the Willaumez Peninsula. On our last diving day, we
arrived to find a tiny island surrounded by a carpet of delicate corals and
volcanoes on the far horizon. I was completely mesmerized by the scene
in front of me, when a father and son in their outrigger glided past in
absolute silence.

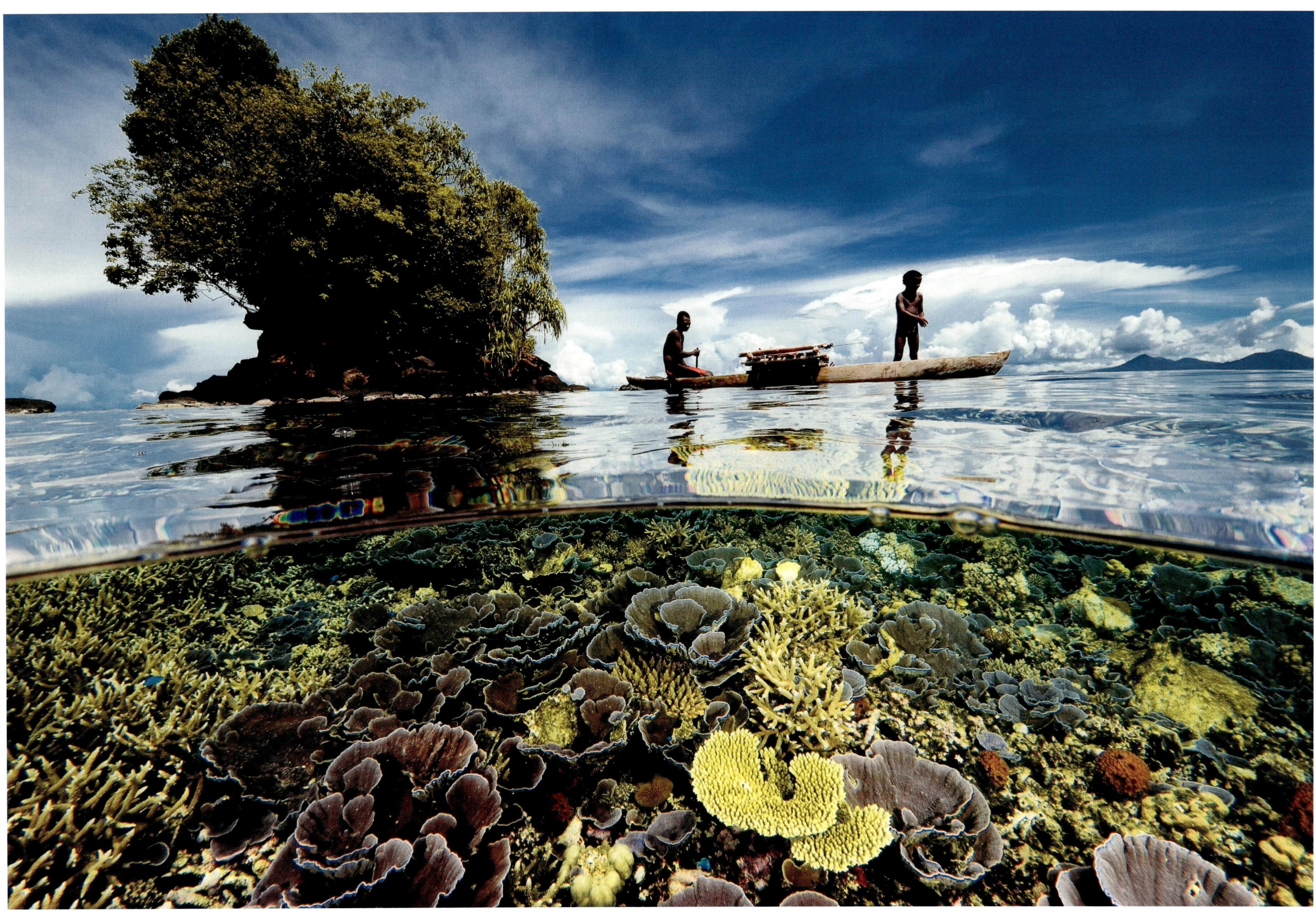

Kawanishi H8K2, Rabaul, Papua New Guinea, 1986

The wreckage of a Japanese Kawanishi H8K2 flying boat in Simpson
Harbour lies offshore beyond Rabaul's Lakunai Airfield. Over time it
evolved from a relic of war to an underwater playground for local children.
Much of Rabaul and its harbour, including this Second World War
wreck, was buried under layers of ash from the 1994 eruption of nearby
Mount Tavurvur.

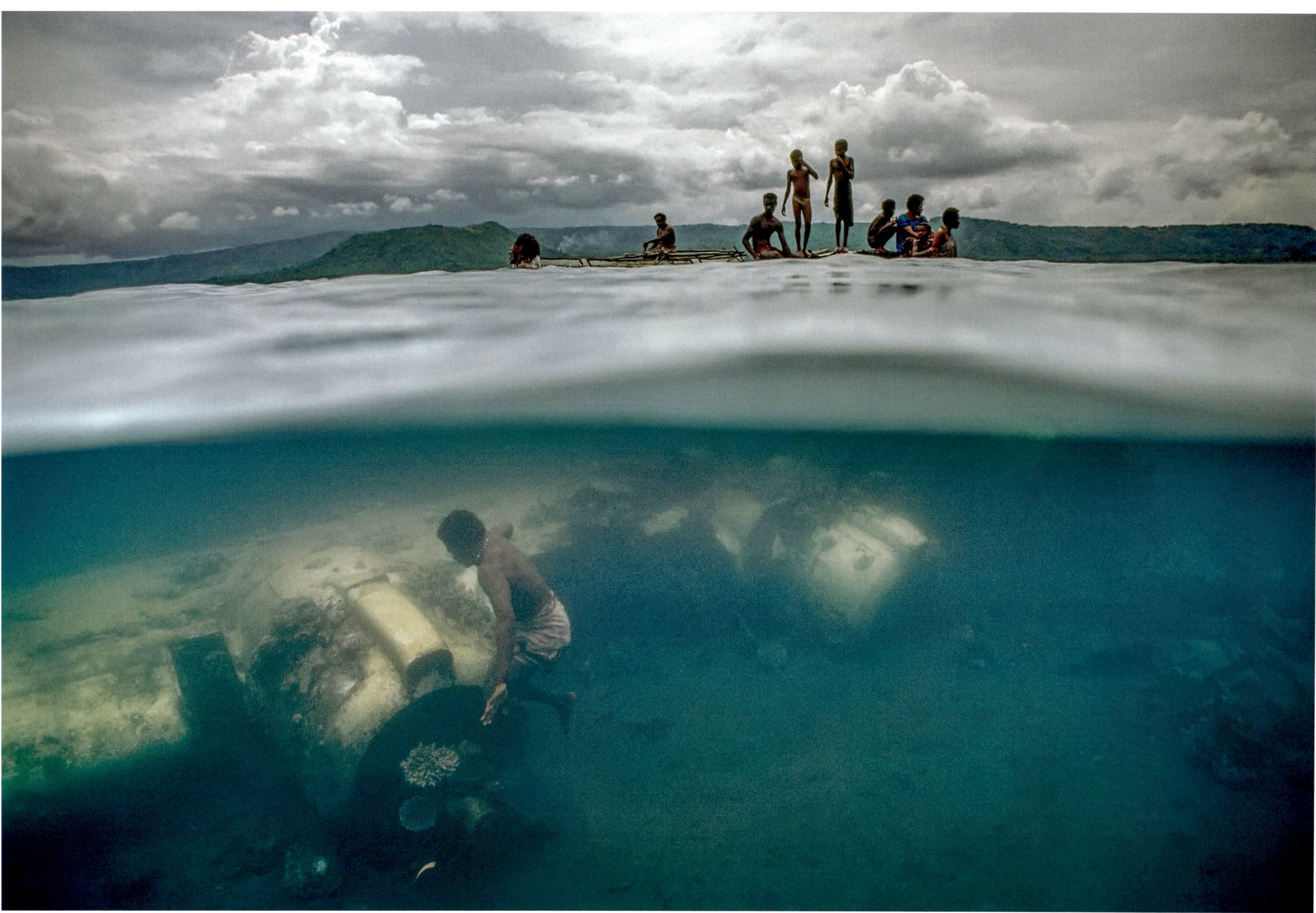

Green Sea Turtle Hatchling, Marutea Atoll, French Polynesia, 1996

A green sea turtle hatchling (*Chelonia mydas*) swims for the open sea beneath a Polynesian-blue sky. Few of these tiny reptiles will survive to become ancient mariners, swimming thousands of miles in their decades-long lifetimes. If this turtle is male, he will never touch shore again. If a female, she will return to her nesting beach to lay her own clutch of eggs. Already struggling, sea turtle populations face new challenges related to climate change as the seas rise and flood their nests. Warmer sands also produce fewer males, which has a damaging impact on breeding numbers.

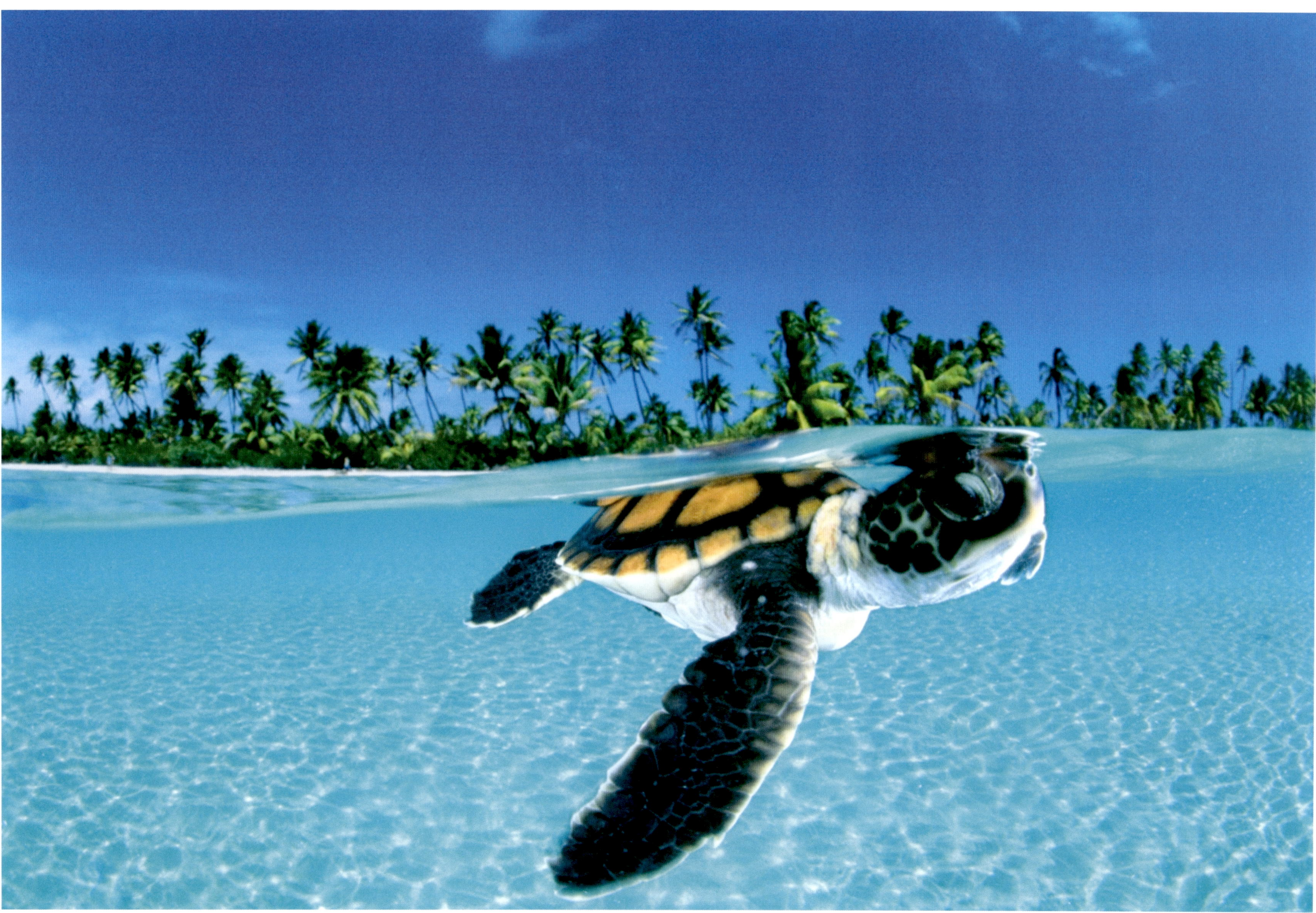

South Pass, Fakarava Atoll, French Polynesia, 2018

A setting sun paints the sky above the South Pass connecting the
lagoon and the open sea on Fakarava Atoll. Hidden below, a watchful
titan triggerfish (*Balistoides viridescens*) is wary of my presence on
the coral drop off that he shares with a host of other reef fish. As the
sun sets, the fish will seek cover for the long, predator-filled night ahead.

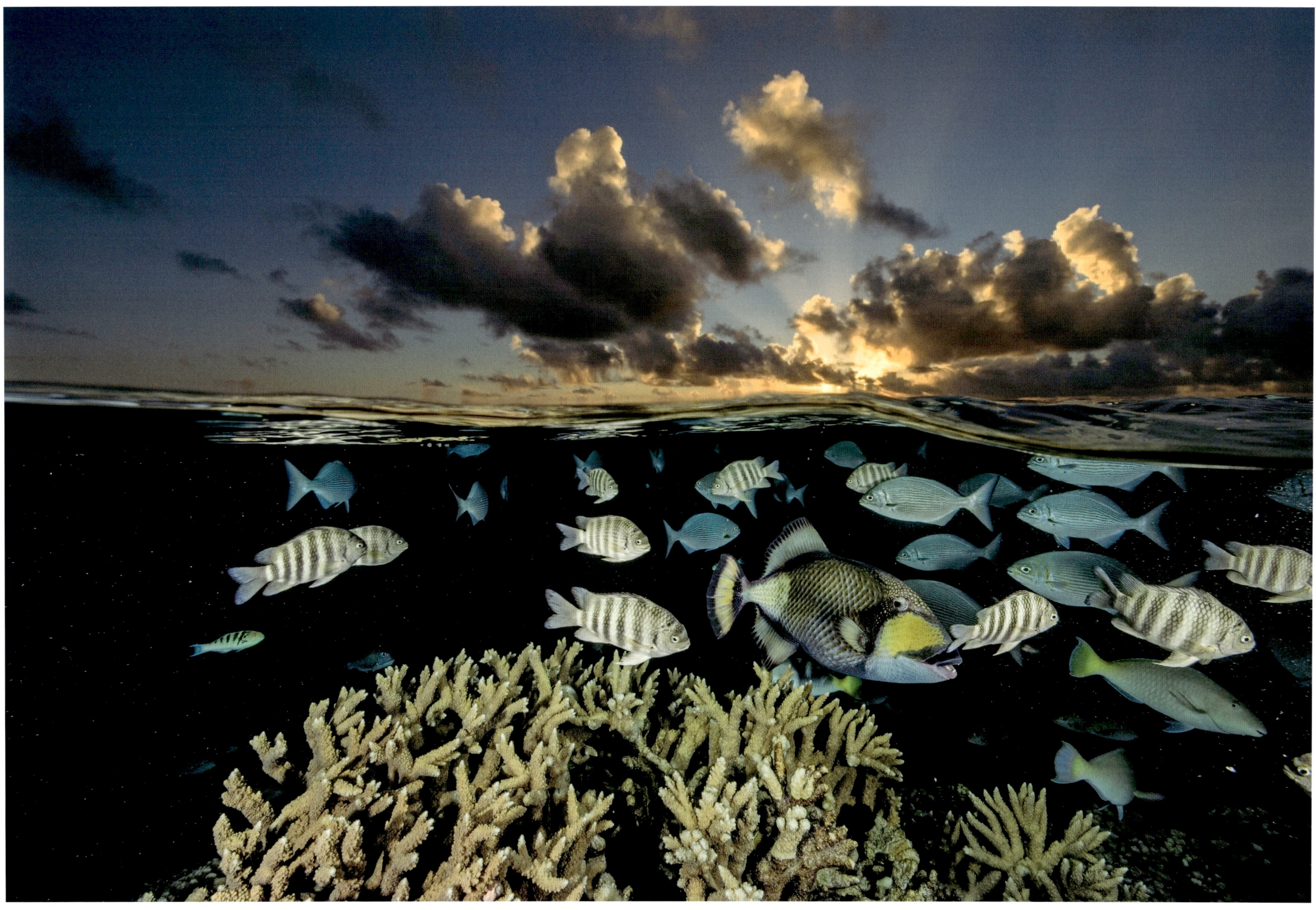

**Blacktip Reef Sharks, South Pass, Fakarava Atoll,
French Polynesia, 2018**

Blacktip reef sharks (*Carcharhinus melanopterus*) patrol the shallow
reefs beneath a glowing Polynesian sunset in South Pass, Fakarava
Atoll. The pass is home to an estimated 700 sharks, one of the densest
populations of predators on the planet. It is a place where small sharks
busy themselves in the shallows that gradually slope to a canyon where,
by day, squadrons of grey reef sharks soar like fighter planes in the stiff
current. At dusk, the sharks gather to hunt the reef. Hundreds flow like
a river above, through and below the coral, looking for fish desperately
trying not to be found. Diving here at night is a rare window into sharks'
secret lives and their struggle to survive.

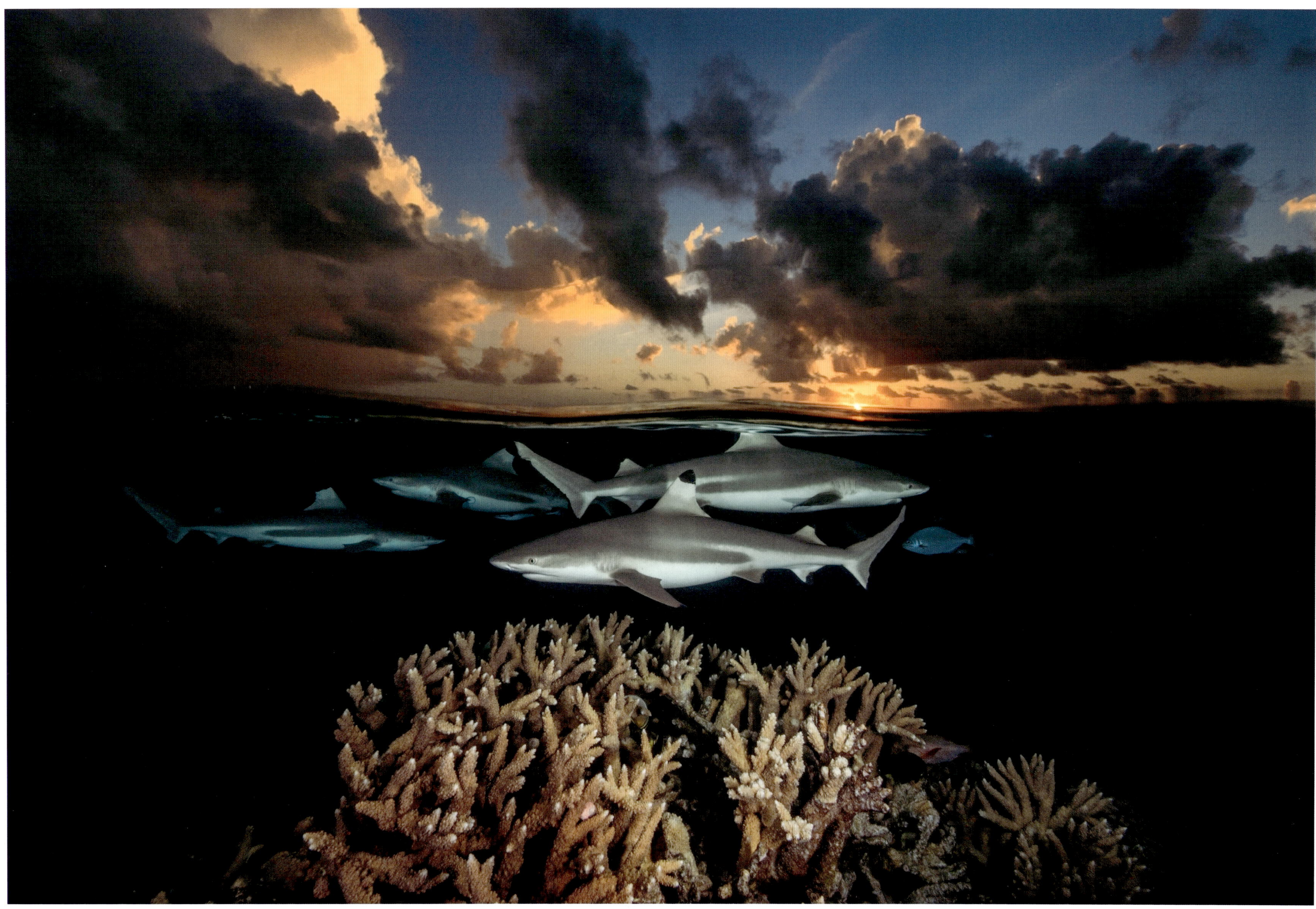

Rodefjord, Scoresby Sund, Greenland, 2015

We entered an iceberg graveyard in Rodefjord, in eastern Greenland,
where towering islands of ice had grounded on the seabed. It was a maze
of sculptures, each one different to the other. The late sun began to dip
behind a wind-worn iceberg. I waited and watched as the water lit up,
and the ice glowed like a giant sapphire in the sea for a few short minutes
before the sun vanished, leaving cold shadows behind.

Nordvestfjord, Scoresby Sund, Greenland, 2015
(overleaf, left and right)

Brooding September skies reflect the mysterious underworld of icebergs
that appear to flow from the glacier valley and plunge into the fjord.
The retreat of the Daugaard-Jensen glacier produces a sequestered sea
of icebergs here that remain secret and unseen in the Nordvestfjord. It
is difficult to describe what it is like to submerge into this farthest-reaching
branch of Scoresby Sund, the world's largest and longest fjord guarded
by mountains reaching 2,000 metres (6,500 feet) in height.

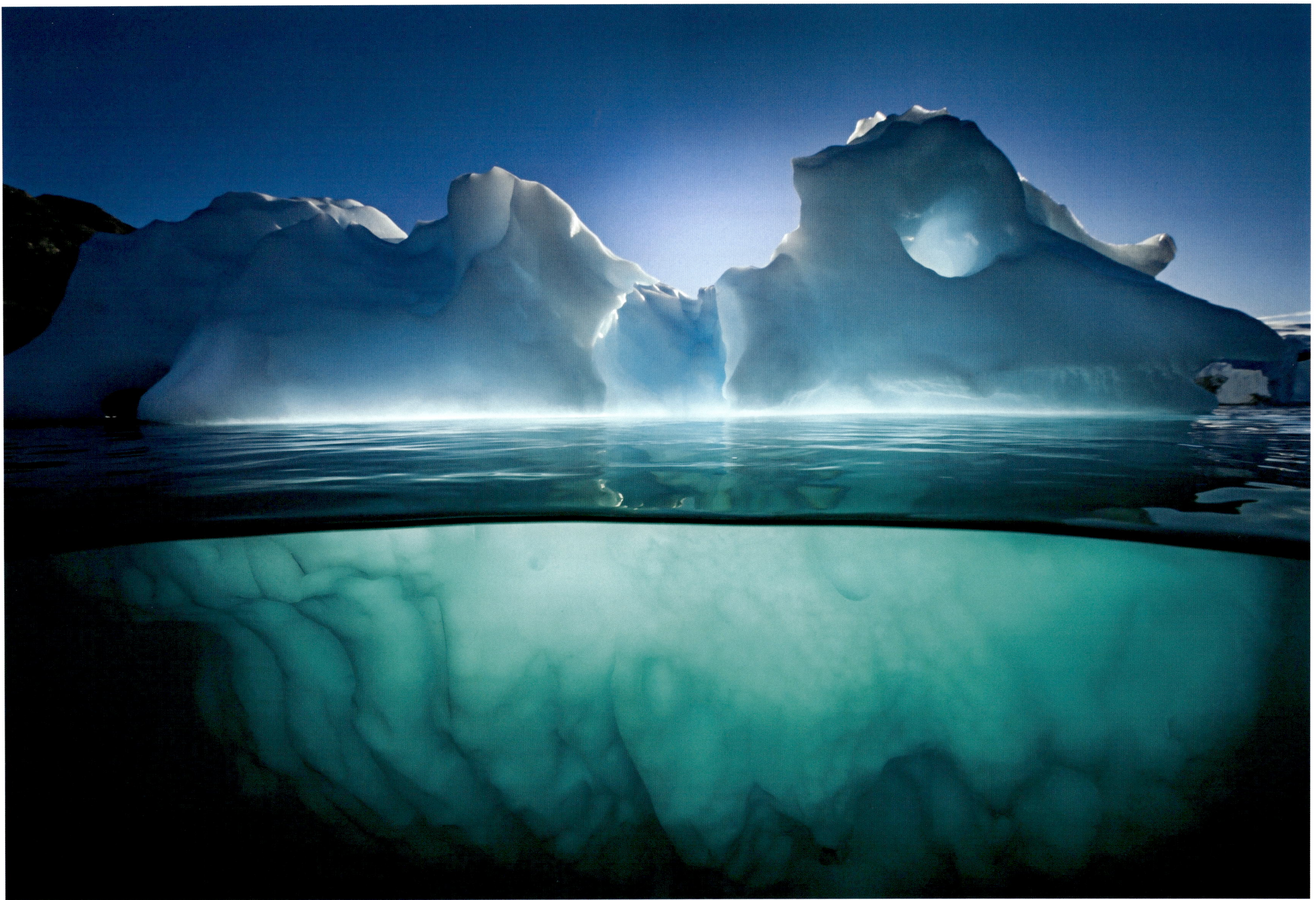

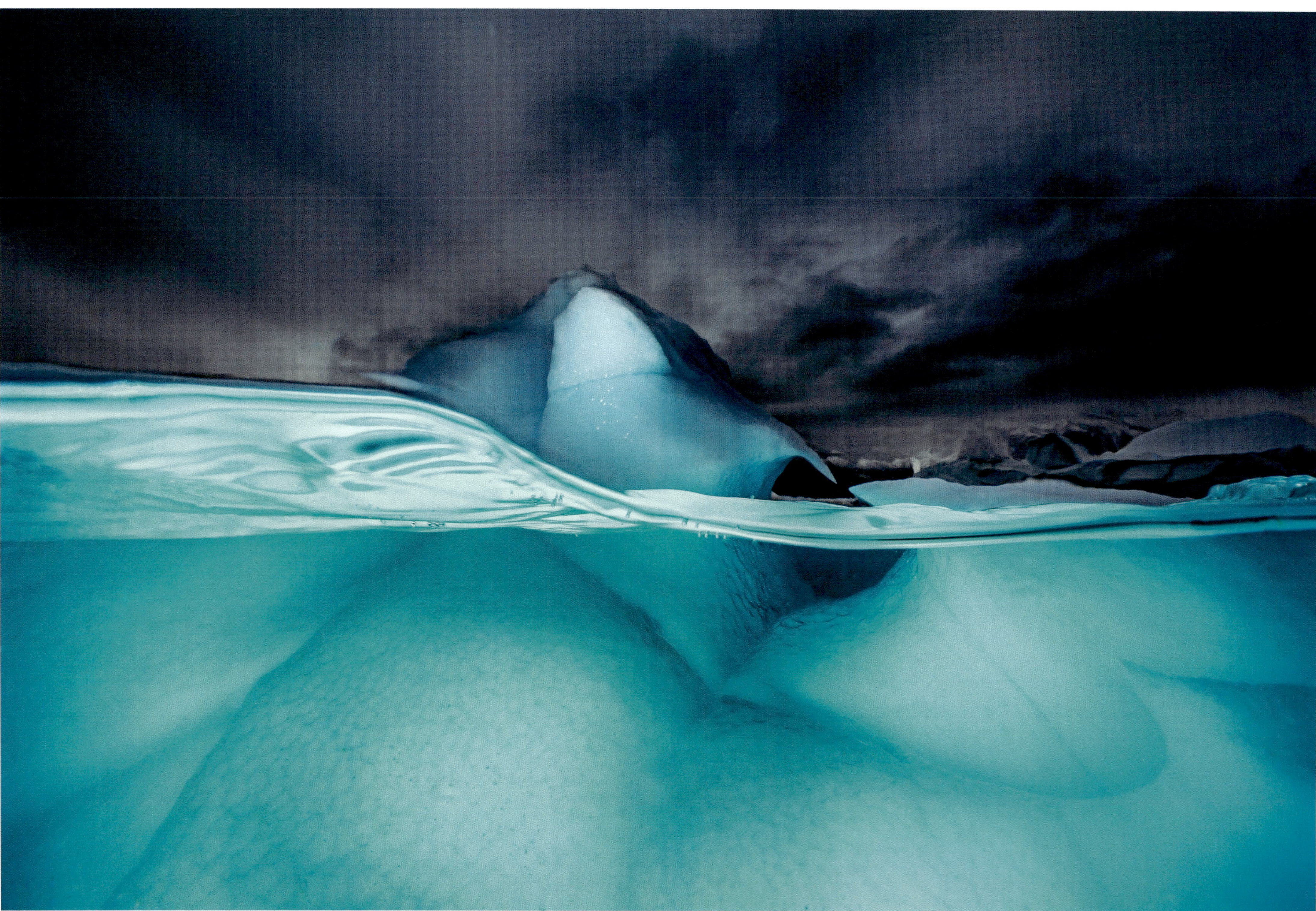

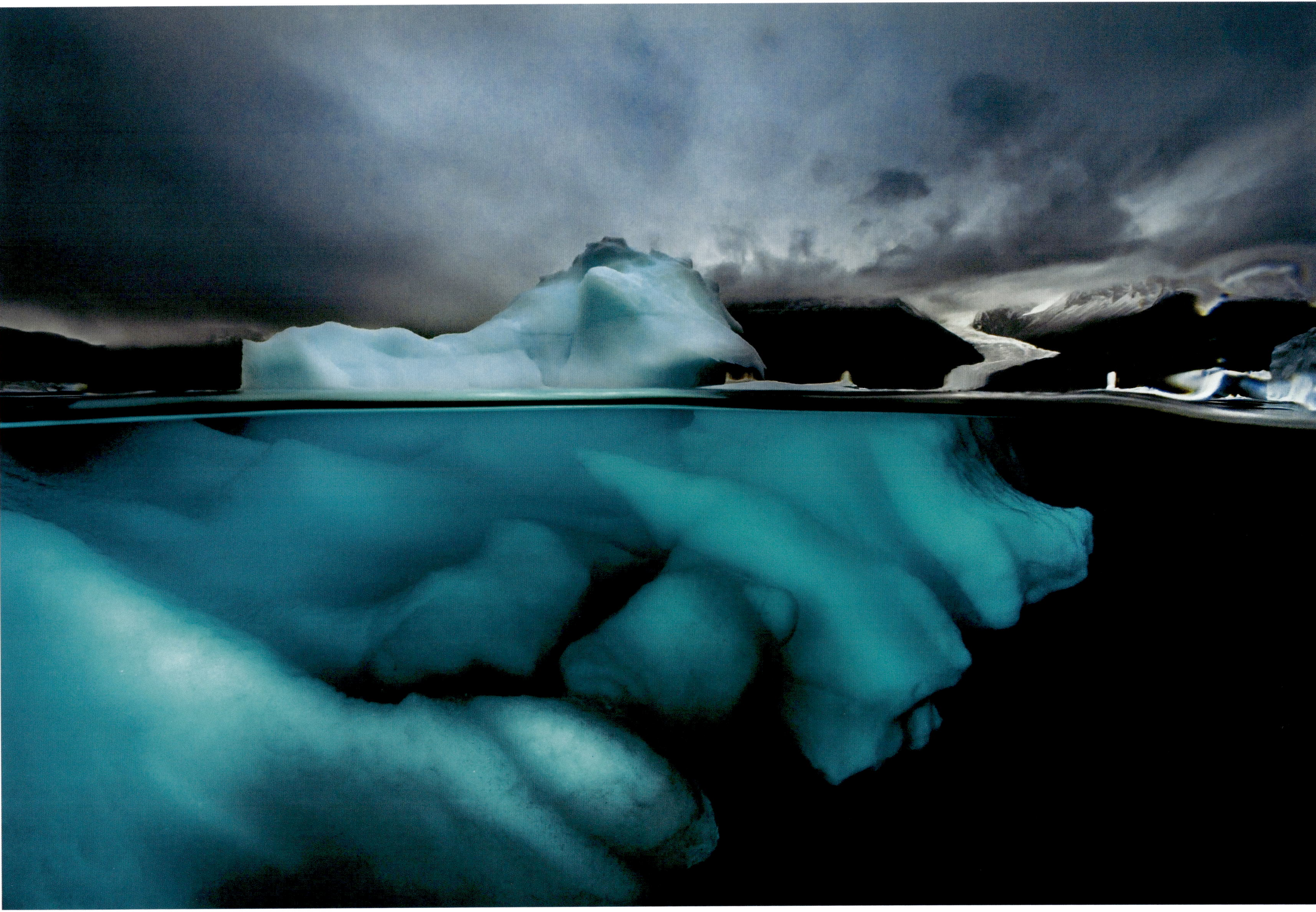

Bowdoin Fjord, Greenland, 2018

A large, textured iceberg in Bowdoin Fjord, in northwest Greenland, seduced me to swim toward it. I discovered a deep vestibule beckoning inward. Keeping a safe distance, I used a powerful flash to concentrate and reflect light inside the ultra-white Arctic chamber, producing an unexpected and unearthly beam that spilled back into the sea.

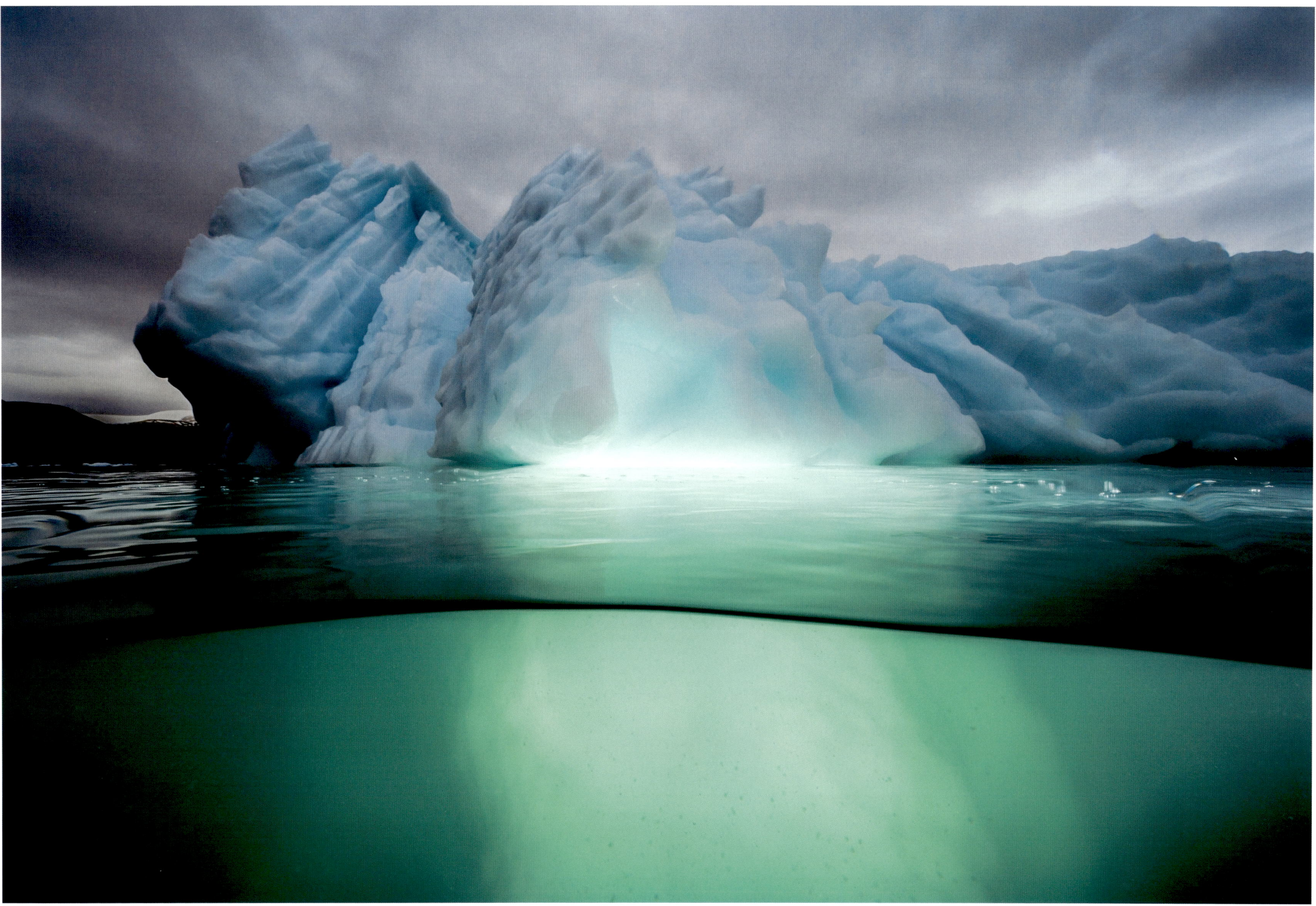

Grounded Iceberg, Blanley Bay, Devon Island, Nunavut, Canada, 2018

A once-mighty iceberg has come to rest in the shallows of Blanley Bay,
on the southern shore of Devon Island in the Canadian Arctic. The ice stood
out like a lone white statue against the empty landscape of the largest
uninhabited island in the world. Sculpted by wind and wave, the ice was
changing in front of me as I swam around it. It would soon vanish into
the sea entirely.

Melville Bay, Greenland, 2018 (overleaf)

A majestic iceberg reflects the size and shape of the nearby mountains
in northwest Greenland's Melville Bay. As I explored and photographed
this giant, I became mesmerized by its secrets. The visible surface sloped
into a gentle saddle, but its flanks plunged unforgivingly into the dark
and unknown depths below me. As impressive as its size was a profound
humming sound rising from deep within the ice, spreading through the
water like an echo of a distant symphony.

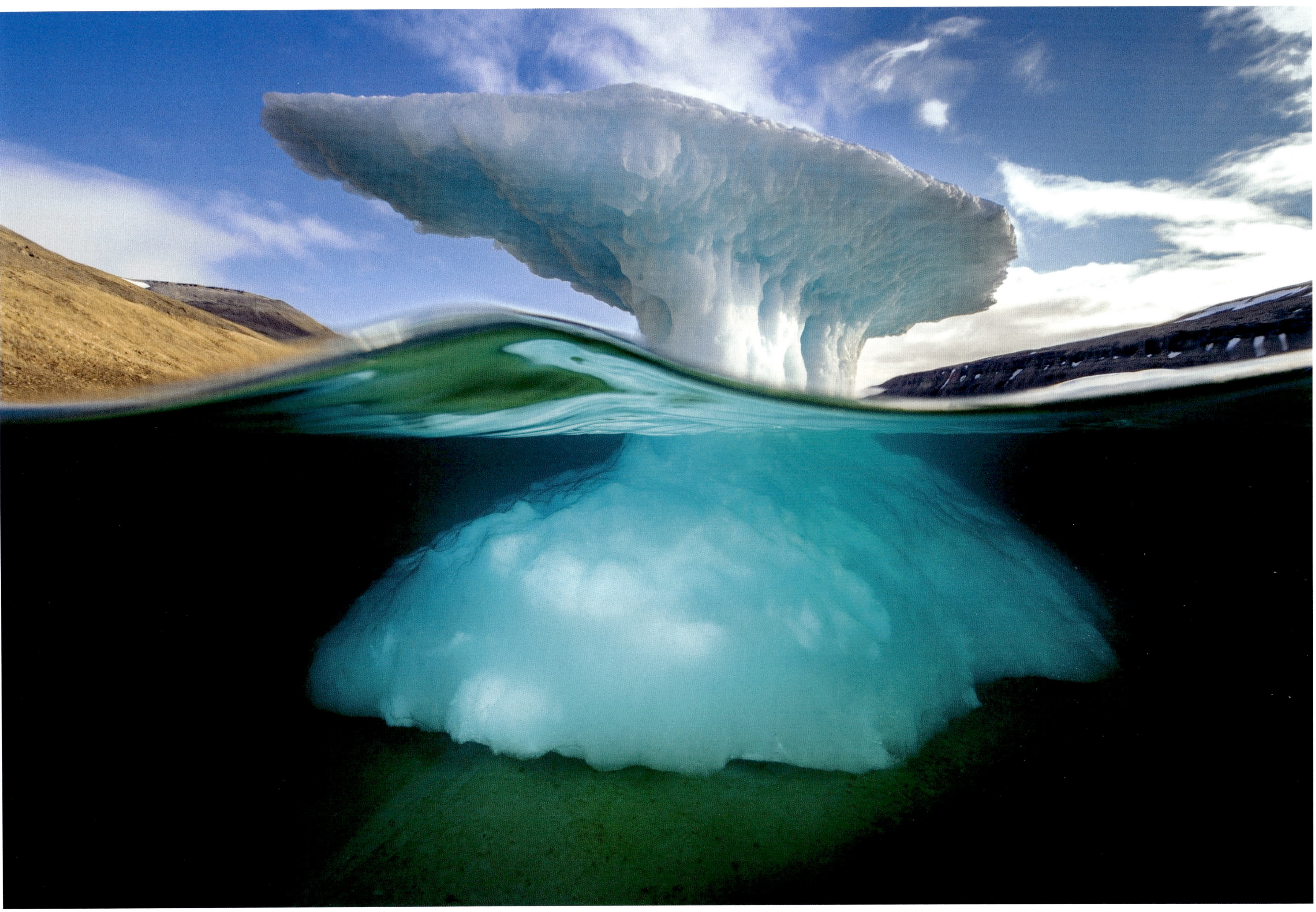

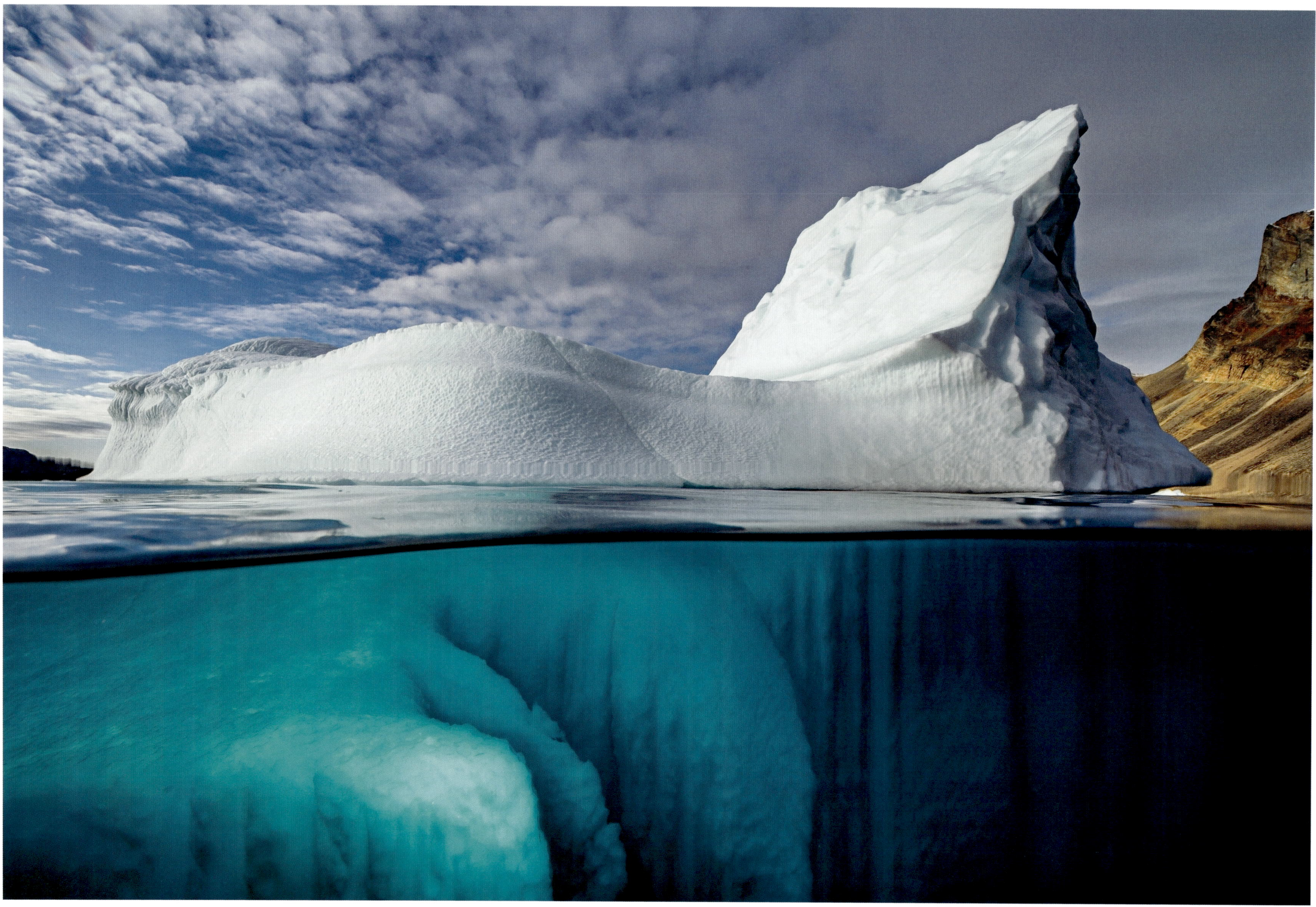

Photographs are wondrous things. They stop time, allowing us to observe closely, think deeply and, one hopes, understand what we see more clearly. They also transcend space, taking us to places we have never visited and places humankind may never reach, such as distant galaxies. The best of them do more than simply show us new sights or amuse us for a moment. They take us captive, challenge our preconceptions, transform our sense of the world around us, inspire and motivate us.

The images in this collection are spectacular examples of these powers of photography. David's innovative technique freezes the perpetual motion of air and sea, taking us into two worlds simultaneously. The above-water scenes seem familiar, known from picture postcards, if not from direct experience: the gleaming tip of an iceberg, a sailboat on a calm blue sea, the palm-lined shore of a tropical island. They are spare and distant, occupying just a small portion of each frame. The underwater realm is large, dramatic and up-close, and even on a two-dimensional page, stunningly three-dimensional – another wonder of photography.

As I spent more time with David's images, I found they had yet another power. They evoked what we might call the 'overview effect', that shift in perspective – in comprehension – that comes about when you see something long considered familiar in a completely different way. When looking at Earth through a spacecraft window, for example, your everyday sense of who and where we are evaporates instantly when confronted with such a radically different view. You realize that we live on a tiny beach ball, and the insignificance of the hectic, striving, everyday world you left behind becomes clear. You feel a deep sense of connection to the whole Earth and all that lives upon it. The experience fills you with awe and wonder, and you return to Earth with an urge to help create a better world. Ask any astronaut.

Something similar hit me as I pondered these images. At first glance, I saw a dry world separate from a wet one. After a few moments, this grew into a sense of two worlds together. Then, in a flash, I became vividly aware that each is part of the other. These 'two worlds' and all the creatures in them – including us humans – are inextricably linked, interconnected and interdependent. When 'others' come together, they become one.

The importance of this insight cannot be overstated. All life on this planet depends on the ocean. It provides oxygen, delivers life-giving rains and moderates the climate. Since time immemorial, humans have used the world's water, transporting our goods across it and drawing upon it to feed both body and soul. The impact of our uses intensified as our numbers and industrial strength grew, to the point that the ocean's capacity to provide these benefits in the future is now in question.

I hope *Two Worlds* evokes that 'overview' sense of awe, wonder and oneness in everyone who picks it up. These forces can unite people and motivate us to work together to care for our precious oceans and ensure we leave our grandchildren a better world.

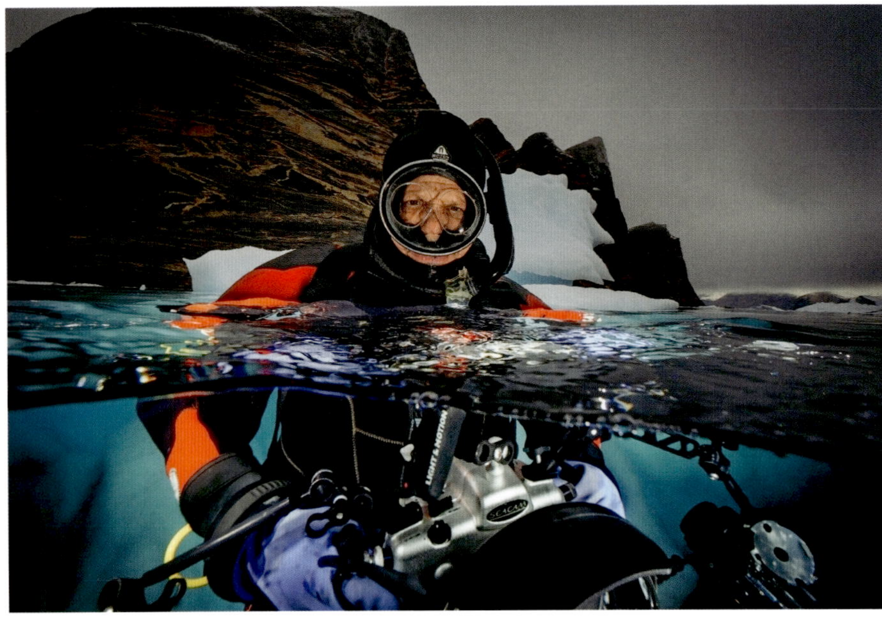

I call them 'half-and-half' pictures. They are also referred to as 'over-unders', 'split' or 'above-and-below' images. Many people ask me: 'Are those pictures real?', 'Are they made in Photoshop?', 'How do you do it?' and 'Do you need a special camera?' To answer the first questions, yes, the pictures are real, and they are not created in Photoshop. To answer the other two questions, let us begin at the beginning.

Creating a successful over-under picture was next to impossible in the early days before advanced underwater housings and super-wide-angle lenses because of light refraction. Light bends when it enters the water and magnifies everything it hits by 33 per cent. Wearing a dive mask and looking at a person waist-deep in the water, they appear normal size above the surface and frighteningly large below – 33 per cent larger to be precise.

I am often credited with creating the over-under image, but that wonderful distinction goes to Coles Phinizy, a *Sports Illustrated* senior editor and photographer who built a single complex camera in the early 1960s that corrected this distortion. He showed me his photographs of Olympic swimmers one day when we met for lunch in New York. I instantly recognized that his design had conquered the optics barrier, and the ability to create a half-and-half image was born with this one custom camera. I often wonder where that camera is now.

The next breakthrough occurred when *National Geographic* photographer Bates Littlehales and optical engineer Gomer McNeill created an underwater camera housing called the OceanEye for the Nikon F. This piece of photo-engineering came with an 8-inch acrylic dome that corrected for that pesky magnification of water. The system was commercially available, so I made an investment and set out across the planet on assignment in Ceylon (now Sri Lanka). The OceanEye and its Nikon interchangeable lenses meant that I could photograph everything from sharks to shipwrecks and also capture two worlds in one frame. I always kept one housing set-up for over-under images with me, just in case I encountered an opportunity, and I became mildly obsessed with linking two worlds on each assignment. Without realizing it was happening, they became a signature image for me, something I was compelled to search out and create wherever I was working.

In the years B.D. (Before Digital), we had just 36 measly frames and no chance to correct our mistakes. There was no margin for error and experimentation. Worse still, usually, I would not see my slides for three to four months after I shot them. I shudder to recall the screams of anguish and anger emanating from the tiny editing rooms on the eighth floor of the *National Geographic* offices, where we sat surrounded by stacks of yellow Kodak boxes that were loaded one by one into a 'Garret box' (a quick-view slide projection system designed by former editor-in-chief Bill Garrett). Only then, sitting in an office chair, would I discover out-of-focus frames, strobe failure, under-exposed rolls, black frames from stuck shutters, dreaded water droplets on the dome – or a wonderful surprise that would become the centre of the story. Thinking about it now, it was no wonder I smoked back then.

The world A.D. (After Digital) is radically different. The most significant game-changers allow creative freedom, such as endless card capacity and viewing the shots instantaneously. Freed from the tyranny of 36 frames, photographers were suddenly able to experiment, succeed, fail, see and learn in real time. Today, I descend with a range of Nikon cameras in state-of-the-art Seacam housings, handmade with precision craftsmanship by the brilliant Austrian engineer Harald Hordosch. I like to be prepared for anything. There is nothing worse than swimming into an incredible scene and not having the right equipment to capture a fleeting ocean moment. The most important lesson I have learned is that you rarely get a second chance in the sea. Always be ready.

Optically, over-under images require a large dome that spreads the boundary layer of water and air across its surface, and the larger the dome, the better. I use a 9½-inch optical glass superdome for most assignments because it packs and swims well. Photographing two worlds is really photographing a wide-angle seascape and landscape simultaneously, which requires a super-wide-angle lens behind the dome. I rely on a range of Nikon lenses, including a 14–24mm f/2.8 mm, 16–35mm f/4 and the 16mm f/2.8 fish-eye that works well in a world without straight lines.

For these images to work, however, both the surface and below need to be in focus. I photograph at or near f/22 for maximum depth of field and let natural light illuminate the surface. I like to let the sky produce the drama and mood of a picture, whether it is a brilliant Polynesian-blue morning or grey, brooding Antarctic afternoon. I am always drawn to the last touch of light, when the sky alone becomes the surface subject. I stand or kneel carefully if the bottom is not delicate, or better yet, float with the dome half-submerged and set the shutter speed to expose for the surface. At midday, I hover around 1/125th second, and as dusk approaches, I may photograph at ½ second. This is a good time to experiment with late light and reflections on the underside of the sea. I use many combinations of Sea & Sea strobes to add light underwater.

Surprisingly, the greatest challenge is often not technical at all. It is the task of finding the subjects and moments that tell a compelling story where the image above is complementing the drama below. I love making these pictures, but they are few and far between. There is unpredictable magic in the molecular border of the surface, and the best images have a way of drawing you into the sea and telling the story of these two worlds.

Two Worlds: Above and Below the Sea
is dedicated to my brother in the sea:

Leandro Blanco Ramirez

Every click of the shutter is a collaboration.

I am sincerely grateful for professional and personal relationships that shape who I am, how I work in the sea and how I share that vision. The *National Geographic* team and Rolex have provided me the perspective of decades of time in the sea. Thank you Francesco Raeli, Lionel Schurch, Jean-Frédéric Dufour and the Rolex New York team.

My colleagues at *National Geographic*, I thank you for your commitment to editorial excellence, our story-telling journey and support: Susan Goldberg, Whitney Johnson, Kathy Moran, Sarah Leen, Sadie Quarrier, Elizabeth Krist, Susan Welchman, Chris Johns, David Griffin, Emory Kristof, Kenji Yamaguchi, Joe Stancampiano, Charlene Valeri and Tom O'Brien.

A story is as strong as its science. Thank you for advancing our understanding of the sea: Dr Eugenie Clark, Dr Sylvia Earle, Dr Harold (Doc) Edgerton, Dr David Fridman, Dr Sonny Gruber, Dr Mike Hammill, Dr William Hamner, Dr Peter Harrison and Dr Charlie Veron.

I am honoured and lucky to collaborate with those who demand excellence in their disciplines: Hal Silverman at Silverman studio, Harald Hordosch at Seacam, Goran Ehlme at Waterproof, Alan Edmonds at Henderson Aquatics, Dan Humble at Dive Tech, Sea & Sea and Fourth Element.

Expeditions are the heart of exploration, discovery and documenting the most important story on Earth – Earth Itself. I am honoured to have descended beneath the Arctic, Antarctic and Pacific waters with Michael Aw and the Elysium Expeditions. It has been a joy to join the unparalleled leader in global expeditions, Sven-Olaf Lindblad, and members of his team: Captain Oliver Kruess, Lisa Kelley, Dennis Cornejo, Paul North and the remaining staff and crew behind the *National Geographic* Lindblad Fleet.

I would like to extend gratitude across the seas to my colleagues:
Australia: Gary Bell, Rodney Fox, Great Barrier Reef Legacy, Karen Gowlett-Holmes, Chris Jones, John Rumney
Bermuda: Philippe Rouja, Jean-Pierre Rouja, Teddy, Edna and Wendy Tucker
Botswana, Okavango Delta: Colin Bell, Brad and Andy Bestelink, Beverly and Dereck Joubert
Canada, Gulf of St Lawrence: Danielle Alary, Paul Boissinot, Mario Cyr, Denis Eloquin, Michel Gilbert, Gros Morne National Park, Hotels Accents, Rick Stanley, John Taylor
Cayman Islands: Sunset House
Commonwealth of Bahamas: Jim Abernathy, Jonathan Bird, Scott Smith
Cuba: Wayne Hasson, Noel Lopez, Giuseppe Omegna
French Polynesia, Fakarava Atoll: Bernard Rickenbach, Tetamanu Diving
Guam: Dr Laurie Raymundo, Tim Rock
Japan: Koji Nakamura
Papua New Guinea: The Max Benjamin Family at Walindi Plantation, Alan Raabe
Philippines: Aiyanar Dive Resort, Atlantis Dive Resort, Vina Concepcion, Marissa Floirendo, Lynn Funkhouser, Tet Lara, Angelique Songco, Gutsy Tuason, Patsy Zobel De Ayala
Republic of Indonesia, Raja Ampat: Dr Gerry Allen, Max Ammer, Dr Mark Erdmann
Republic of Palau: Tova Harel, Udi Bornovski, Navot Bornovski
USA: Loggerhead Marine Center, Florida

Thank you to Kathy Sullivan for breaking barriers in two worlds. To Kathy Moran for being a lighthouse in both calm and stormy seas. To my book agent Robin Strauss. To Victoria Clarke and Jane Ace for editorial guidance, Anna Rieger for her beautiful design, Elaine Ward and Jane Harman for their excellent colour work.

Jennifer Hayes, one word: Everything.

David Doubilet (b.1946) is a contributing photographer and author for *National Geographic* magazine, who has produced over 75 publications ranging from the equator to beneath the polar ice. He enters the ocean as a journalist, artist and explorer to document the beauty and devastation in our waters. Doubilet has spent over 27,000 hours capturing a hidden world beneath the surface since he first put his Brownie Hawkeye camera in an anaesthetist's rubber bag at the age of 12. He believes that photography has the power to educate, honour, humiliate, illuminate and influence change.

Doubilet is the recipient of many esteemed photographic awards, including the Academy of Achievement Award, the Lennart Nilsson Award and the Explorers Club Lowell Thomas Award. He is a NOGI Fellow, a member of both the Royal Photographic Society and a founding member of the International League of Conservation Photographers. Doubilet is honoured to have been a Rolex Testimonee since 1994.

Kathy Moran is *National Geographic* magazine's Deputy Director of Photography. As the magazine's first senior editor for natural history projects, Moran has been producing projects about terrestrial and underwater ecosystems for the magazine since 1990. She is a founding member of the International League of Conservation Photographers and has edited numerous books for ILCP photographers published with the University of Chicago Press.

Kathryn D. Sullivan is an American geologist and a former NASA astronaut. A crew member on three Space Shuttle missions, she became the first American woman to walk in space on 11 October 1984. On 7 June 2020, she became the first woman to dive to the Challenger Deep in the Mariana Trench, the deepest part of the Earth's oceans. From 2014 to 2017, she served as Under Secretary of Commerce for Oceans and Atmosphere, and Administrator of the National Oceanic and Atmospheric Administration.

Phaidon Press Limited
2 Cooperage Yard
London E15 2QR

Phaidon Press Inc.
65 Bleecker Street
New York, NY 10012

phaidon.com

First published 2021
Reprinted 2022
© 2021 Phaidon Press Limited
Photographs and text © David Doubilet

ISBN 978 1 83866 318 6
ISBN 978 1 83866 400 8 (signed edition)

A CIP catalogue record for this book is available from the
British Library and the Library of Congress.

Commissioning Editor: Victoria Clarke
Production: Elaine Ward and Jane Harman
Design: Anna Rieger

Printed in China

Front cover: **Opal Reef, Great Barrier Reef, Australia, 2009** (page 71)
Back cover: **Chinstrap and Gentoo Penguins, Danco Island,
Antarctica, 2011** (page 9)